THE ABBOT'S GREAT SACRIFICE

The pleasures that bridge can bring are well known – the joy of winning, the satisfaction of bidding a fine slam or finding the one defence to beat an opponent's contract. It can also be the most frustrating of games. Hopeless opponents stumble into a good contract, or completely misplay a game and still manage to make it. In this eighth collection of stories featuring the bridge-crazy monks of St Titus, the pompous and self-important Abbot suffers more than his fair share of the game's aggravations. The world's worst house guest, Brother Herman from Australia, pays the monastery a visit. A team of attractive young girls arrives at the monastery, playing unexpectedly well and drawing unwarranted attention from the virile novices. A disastrous start sends the Abbot to the bottom row of a Swiss Teams, where he receives an unrequired lecture on Restricted Choice from the 80-year-old Elsie Bonneville.

David Bird is the world's leading writer of humorous bridge fiction and his followers can look forward to another top-class mixture of exhilarating bridge and true-to-life characterisation and dialogue.

THE ABBOT'S
GREAT SACRIFICE

David Bird

CASSELL
in association with
PETER CRAWLEY

First published in Great Britain 2003
in association with Peter Crawley
by Cassell
Wellington House, 125 Strand, London WC2R 0BB
an imprint of the Orion Publishing Group Ltd

A catalogue record for this book
is available from the British Library

ISBN 0 304 36613 7

Typeset at The Spartan Press Ltd,
Lymington, Hants

Printed in Great Britain by
Clays Ltd, St Ives plc

Contents

My thanks go to Tim Bourke, a close friend and fellow author, who gave me many of the best deals in this book.   DB.

1. The Abbot's Change of Heart

The Abbot had never been able to make up his mind whether to allow novices to play in the weekly duplicate. They were a reliable source of tops, in the main, but nothing was more frustrating than a young pair stumbling into a good board against him. Even worse, they tended to make a note of the hand, knowing they would find a ready audience when they returned to the novitiate. The Abbot sighed heavily. Ah well, it was his duty as spiritual leader to instruct the flock by playing in expert fashion against them. Any occasional moment of aggravation must be borne with fortitude.

'Good evening, Abbot,' said Brother Adam, taking his seat. 'I hope you and Brother Xavier are well.'

At least these two are polite, thought the Abbot. That Brother Cameron was the worst culprit. How could he show no respect at all to someone who was forty years his senior? It defied all reason. 'We're very well, thank you,' he replied. 'Have you found tonight's session beneficial?'

'I made a silly mistake on the last hand, I'm afraid,' said Brother Adam. 'I miscounted trumps.'

'We never seem to play very well against Lucius and Paulo,' added Brother Mark. 'We get nervous against strong players.'

The Abbot peered at the novice. If there was any nervousness to be displayed it should be at his table, not at Brother Lucius's.

The players drew their cards for the first board of the round:

North-South game
Dealer West

```
                    ♠ A Q 7
                    ♡ 6 4 3
                    ◇ K Q 7 5 4
                    ♣ 4 2
    ♠ J 9 5                          ♠ 10 6 4 3
    ♡ K Q 10 9 7 2        N          ♡ –
    ◇ 9              W         E      ◇ J 10 8 6 2
    ♣ A Q 8              S           ♣ 10 9 7 5
                    ♠ K 8 2
                    ♡ A J 8 5
                    ◇ A 3
                    ♣ K J 6 3
```

WEST	NORTH	EAST	SOUTH
The	*Brother*	*Brother*	*Brother*
Abbot	*Mark*	*Xavier*	*Adam*
1♡	2◇	Pass	3NT
All Pass			

The Abbot led the king of hearts against 3NT and surveyed Brother Mark's dummy with disapproval. What an appalling vulnerable over-call! He would doubtless have been too nervous to make such an overcall against Brother Lucius. Still, with any luck Xavier would hold something good in diamonds and the contract would go down. How was declarer taking it? Did he look disappointed?

'Nice hand, partner,' said Brother Adam. 'Thank you.'

Brother Xavier discarded a club on the first trick and the novice allowed the Abbot's king of hearts to win. It was not attractive to continue hearts into the tenace and the Abbot switched to a low spade. The young declarer won with the king and played the ace and king of diamonds, the Abbot throwing a heart on the second round.

'Oh dear, that's unlucky,' said Brother Adam.

It's no more than they deserve, thought the Abbot. Overcalling on hands like that was similar to passing rude notes around a classroom – something that you soon grew out of.

Brother Adam cashed dummy's last diamond winner and continued with two more rounds of spades. This position had been reached:

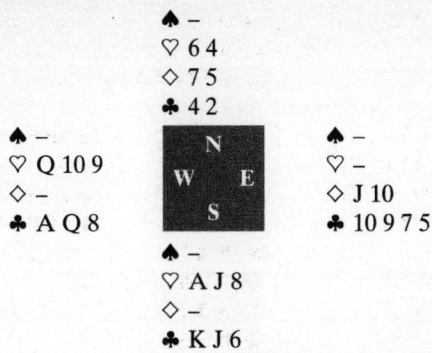

```
          ♠ –
          ♡ 6 4
          ◊ 7 5
          ♣ 4 2
♠ –                        ♠ –
♡ Q 10 9      N            ♡ –
◊ –        W     E         ◊ J 10
♣ A Q 8       S            ♣ 10 9 7 5
          ♠ –
          ♡ A J 8
          ◊ –
          ♣ K J 6
```

When a low heart was played to the eight, the Abbot won with the nine and paused to consider his return. A heart was obviously no good. It looked best to try the queen of clubs. Unless the youngster had a full sixteen-count, Xavier would hold the king or jack of clubs.

Brother Adam won the club queen with the king and sat back in his chair, uncertain how to continue. How many hearts did the Abbot still have? He had discarded two hearts and there had been two rounds of the suit. So, he had two hearts left and he must have two clubs with them. Yes!

Brother Adam played the ace of hearts followed by the jack. The Abbot won with the queen, cashed the ace of clubs and – at Trick 13 – led the club eight. He could not believe it when Brother Adam won with the jack. The game had been made.

'Wow!' exclaimed Brother Mark. 'I don't think I've ever done a throw-in, myself. You did two of them on one hand.'

The Abbot thrust his cards back into the wallet. It was absolutely typical of his luck. This young lad hands a top to Brother Lucius, not even managing to count trumps correctly. He then comes to his table and totters towards the winning play as if guided by some missile control system.

'What are you doing?' demanded the Abbot.

'Er . . . I was just making a note of the hand,' Brother Adam replied. 'Is that all right?'

'We have another board to play,' declared the Abbot. 'Do you want to keep the whole room waiting, just so you can brag about some lucky board?'

'Of course not, Abbot.'

'Appalling lack of consideration,' continued the Abbot. 'For a moment I thought I was playing against Brother Cameron.'

A round or two later, Brother Aelred arrived at the Abbot's table. His usual partner, Brother Michael, was visiting a sick relative and he had formed a makeshift partnership with the black-bearded Brother Zac. This was the first board of the round:

Game all
Dealer East

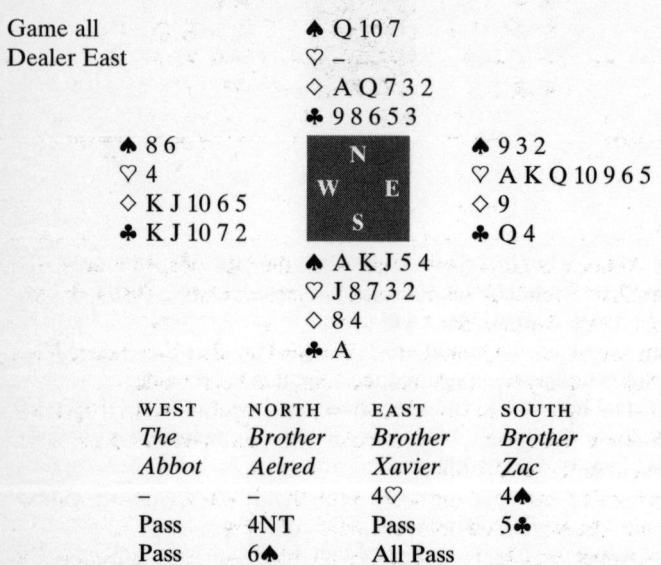

♠ Q 10 7
♡ –
◇ A Q 7 3 2
♣ 9 8 6 5 3

♠ 8 6
♡ 4
◇ K J 10 6 5
♣ K J 10 7 2

♠ 9 3 2
♡ A K Q 10 9 6 5
◇ 9
♣ Q 4

♠ A K J 5 4
♡ J 8 7 3 2
◇ 8 4
♣ A

WEST	NORTH	EAST	SOUTH
The	*Brother*	*Brother*	*Brother*
Abbot	*Aelred*	*Xavier*	*Zac*
–	–	4♡	4♠
Pass	4NT	Pass	5♣
Pass	6♠	All Pass	

The Abbot led his singleton heart and shook his head in disbelief when the dummy appeared. 'You bid Blackwood with a void?' he queried.

'No, it was Roman Key-card Blackwood,' Brother Aelred replied. 'My partner's response showed three aces or two aces and the king of trumps. In theory it could be no aces, of course, but since he . . .'

'I'm perfectly familiar with the responses,' snapped the Abbot. 'It's not normal practice to bid 4NT when you have a void. That was my point.'

'I could hardly pass, could I?' persisted Brother Aelred. 'Not with three ruffing values, a trump honour, and such good diamonds.'

'No, indeed,' said Brother Zac. 'Ruff, please.'

Brother Zac crossed to his hand with the ♣A and ruffed another heart. A club ruff was followed by a third heart ruff. He then reached his hand with a further club ruff and drew trumps. This was the position with one trump still to be drawn:

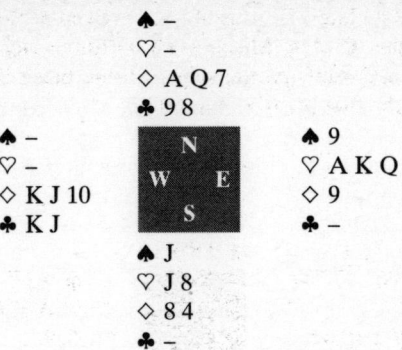

The Abbot was not a happy man when the jack of spades appeared on the table. Eventually he released the jack of clubs. 'Throw the low diamond,' said Brother Zac.

A finesse of the ◇Q succeeded and Brother Zac then conceded a club trick. Dummy was high and the slam had been made.

'Yes, I thought a slam would be there,' said Brother Aelred. 'I didn't like bidding Blackwood on a void but you have to trust your judgement in these situations.'

Brother Zac surveyed the scene proudly. 'It was a squeeze without the count,' he said. 'You don't see many of those.'

The Abbot was unimpressed. 'Such plays are two a penny,' he declared. 'The text books may rant on about rectifying the count but much of the time it's quite unnecessary.'

'We needed a trump lead, Abbot,' said Brother Xavier. 'That stops one of the ruffs.'

Brother Zac had not been overjoyed at the Abbot's dismissive tone. 'A diamond lead kills the ending too,' he informed him. 'In fact, I can't make it on a club lead either. I wouldn't have the entries to ruff three hearts.'

Brother Xavier nodded. 'That's right,' he said. 'Only a heart lead lets it through.'

The Abbot sank back in his chair. 'Stupid of me,' he said heavily. 'I can't think why I led a singleton in the suit you had bid.'

The penultimate round of the pairs saw the arrival of Brother Cameron at the Abbot's table. It was well known that the novice was on his 'final warning' for poor etiquette. Any further failure to greet the opponents or to thank his partner for the dummy and he would suffer a one-month ban from the senior card room.

'Good evening, Abbot,' said Brother Cameron, affecting a small bow as he pulled back his chair. 'And good evening to you, Brother Xavier. I do hope you are both enjoying the session.'

'All right, all right,' grunted the Abbot. 'No need to overdo it.'

Accustomed to picking up flat 7-counts against Brother Cameron, the Abbot was pleasantly surprised to find himself with a useful 18-count. With any luck he would end at the helm of some testing contract. He could then re-assert his authority with a masterful piece of dummy play. This was the deal:

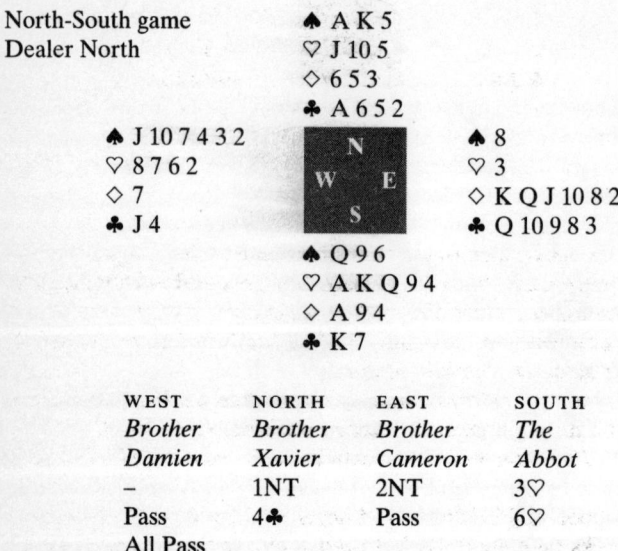

North-South game
Dealer North

North
♠ A K 5
♡ J 10 5
◇ 6 5 3
♣ A 6 5 2

West
♠ J 10 7 4 3 2
♡ 8 7 6 2
◇ 7
♣ J 4

East
♠ 8
♡ 3
◇ K Q J 10 8 2
♣ Q 10 9 8 3

South
♠ Q 9 6
♡ A K Q 9 4
◇ A 9 4
♣ K 7

WEST	NORTH	EAST	SOUTH
Brother	*Brother*	*Brother*	*The*
Damien	*Xavier*	*Cameron*	*Abbot*
–	1NT	2NT	3♡
Pass	4♣	Pass	6♡
All Pass			

Brother Cameron's 2NT showed the minors and ◇7 was led against the eventual heart slam. 'Three good cards for you, Abbot,' observed Brother Xavier. 'I hope it's enough.'

'Play low,' said the Abbot.

Brother Cameron exchanged a glance with his partner. The custom of thanking partner for the dummy was apparently not so universal as the Abbot claimed.

The ten of diamonds appeared from East on the first trick and the Abbot paused for thought. Should he duck the trick, to rectify the count? If Brother Cameron was 5-5 in the minors, this would set up a squeeze. It was slightly dangerous, though, because if the opening lead was a singleton he would suffer a ruff.

The Abbot won with the diamond ace and drew trumps in four rounds. He continued with a fifth round of trumps, throwing a club from dummy, and then turned to the spade suit. This was the position with one spade still to be played:

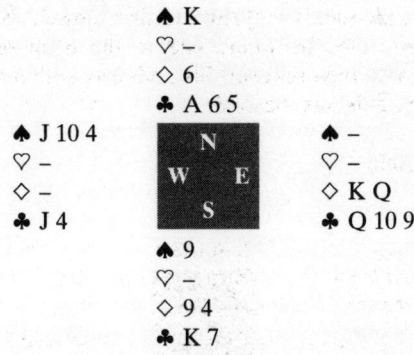

When the spade king was led Brother Cameron had no good card to play. He eventually threw the diamond queen and the Abbot then led a diamond to set up a twelfth trick in the suit.

'A squeeze without the count, as I live and breathe!' exclaimed the Abbot. 'You don't see many of those.'

There was no reaction around the table and Brother Damien stretched out a leg, tapping his partner urgently on the foot.

Brother Cameron jerked into action. 'Very well played, Abbot,' he said.

The Abbot nodded happily. Lucius or Paulo might have made twelve tricks on a good day but no-one else in the monastery would have come close. 'It was a very instructive deal,' he informed Brother Cameron. 'Perhaps you would like to make a note of it.'

'There's another board to play, isn't there?' the novice replied. 'I wouldn't like to hold everyone up.'

'Don't be ridiculous,' declared the Abbot. 'You can't deprive your colleagues of an instructive deal like that. A delay of a minute or two hardly matters at all.'

In a near illegible scrawl Brother Cameron wrote down the hand on the back of his scorecard.

'Don't forget to explain to them that I couldn't rectify the count at Trick 1,' continued the Abbot, raising his voice for the benefit of the adjacent tables. 'A superb play like that . . . well, it should prove an inspiration for the whole novitiate!'

2. Evelyn Butterworth's Brilliancy

The opponents for a Hampshire league match were due to arrive and the Abbot was checking the senior card room. He had turned the heating off a full three hours ago and the temperature had fallen to a satisfactory 59 degrees, confirmed by his pocket match thermometer. This would not inconvenience the monks, who wore plenty of extra layers beneath their cassocks. It should, however, reduce the concentration of the opponents.

Professor Larkley and his team arrived on time and the Abbot ushered them into the card room. 'May I take your coat?' he asked, smiling pleasantly at Sheila Larkley.

'I don't think so,' she replied. 'It's not very warm in here, is it?'

'Better than normal, thanks to the clement weather,' the Abbot replied. 'Most of our funds are devoted to various charities around the world. We don't have much money left for heating, I'm afraid.'

Evelyn Butterworth blew hot air onto her hands. 'I'll keep my coat on too, if you don't mind,' she said.

This was an early board at the Abbot's table.

```
North-South game       ♠ A 8 6 5
Dealer North           ♡ A 9 7 2
                       ◇ 5
                       ♣ Q 6 4 2
     ♠ K Q 10 3                      ♠ J 9 4
     ♡ J 10 8 4          N           ♡ Q 5 3
     ◇ 9            W         E       ◇ K Q J 10 8 4 2
     ♣ J 10 9 7          S           ♣ -
                       ♠ 7 2
                       ♡ K 6
                       ◇ A 7 6 3
                       ♣ A K 8 5 3
```

WEST	NORTH	EAST	SOUTH
Professor	*Brother*	*Sheila*	*The*
Larkley	*Xavier*	*Larkley*	*Abbot*
–	Pass	3◇	Pass
Pass	Dble	Pass	5♣
All Pass			

Professor Larkley, who for several months had not managed to find the time for a haircut, led his singleton diamond against Five Clubs. The Abbot won with the ace and cashed the ace of trumps, noting the 4-0 break. When he continued with a diamond from hand, Professor Larkley paused to consider his defence. There was no point in ruffing, surely? Declarer would overruff with dummy's queen and then play to ruff his remaining diamonds. If West ruffed the third diamond high, declarer would draw the outstanding trump before taking a final diamond ruff in dummy. Concluding that there was unlikely to be a satisfactory defence, the Professor eventually threw a spade.

The Abbot ruffed the diamond in dummy, returned to his hand with the ♡K and led another diamond. Once again the Professor declined to ruff with a trump winner, preferring to throw a spade. The Abbot ruffed cheaply in the dummy and cashed the bare queen of trumps followed by the ace of hearts. If he could score the two low trumps in his hand he would now be home. A heart ruff with the five was followed by a spade to the ace and a fourth round of hearts. East discarded and the Abbot ruffed triumphantly with the eight. 'And the king of trumps makes eleven!' he announced, looking as if he had just eradicated all disease from the universe.

Sheila Larkley was unimpressed. 'Easier in 3NT, isn't it?' she said.

The Abbot could not believe what he was hearing. When Michael-angelo painted the ceiling of the Sistine Chapel did the Pope say to him 'plain white would have been easier'? In any case, how many tricks were there in no-trumps? With the clubs not breaking he would be a trick short, wouldn't he?

'Nine tricks are usually easier than eleven,' continued Sheila Larkley. 'It's one of the first things I learnt.'

'There are only eight tricks in no-trumps,' protested the Abbot. 'The clubs don't break, so I would make four clubs and four outside winners.'

Mrs Larkley waved this objection aside and smiled at her husband. 'Bill and I always go for no-trumps when we have a stopper in the opponents' suit. It works out best in the long run.'

Meanwhile, at the other table, Lucius and Paulo faced the Butter-worths. Evelyn Butterworth was reputed to be an excellent cook and her husband's girth bore witness to this. The players drew their cards for this board:

Love all   ♠ K Q 9 6
Dealer West   ♡ 6 5
                    ♢ 8 5 3
                    ♣ K Q 9 5

♠ 8		♠ J 10 3 2
♡ A Q J 10 9 7 3	N	♡ 4 2
♢ 10 9 7	W E	♢ 6 2
♣ 4 3	S	♣ J 10 8 7 6

                ♠ A 7 5 4
                ♡ K 8
                ♢ A K Q J 4
                ♣ A 2

WEST	NORTH	EAST	SOUTH
Evelyn	*Brother*	*Dennis*	*Brother*
Butterworth	*Paulo*	*Butterworth*	*Lucius*
3♡	Pass	Pass	Dble
Pass	4♠	Pass	6NT
All Pass			

Mrs Butterworth was finding it difficult to handle the cards, wearing gloves. With a determined effort she extracted ♢10. Lucius won with the ace and played the rest of his diamonds, throwing two hearts from dummy. East followed only twice, he was interested to note, and then threw a club and two hearts.

Lucius paused to assess the situation. West had started with 7-3 shape in the red suits, so she would hold only three cards in the black suits. If two of these were in spades, all would be well. The suit would break 3-2 and he would have twelve tricks on top. What if West held only one spade and two clubs? The only chance was to throw East on lead in one black suit, forcing him to concede a trick in the other black suit. For this to be possible, he would have to drop one of the key middle cards from the West hand, setting up a black-suit tenace.

When Brother Lucius cashed the ace and king of clubs West followed twice but neither the jack nor the ten appeared. Lucius crossed his fingers and called for the king of spades. His prayers were answered when the eight of spades dropped from the West hand. East was ripe for a throw-in in this end position:

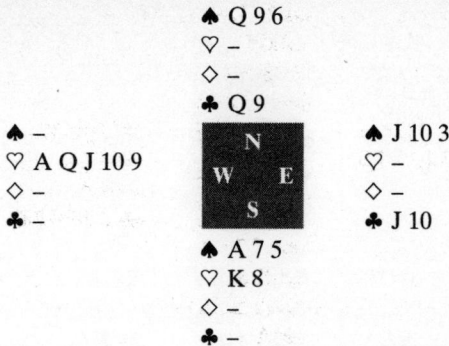

Lucius cashed the queen of clubs, throwing a heart, and exited with a club to East's jack, throwing the king of hearts. When the spade jack was returned, Lucius won with the queen and took the marked finesse of the spade seven. The slam had been made.

'That's a bad one, Dennis,' observed Mrs Butterworth. 'I had the ace of hearts over here. Keep a heart and it goes one down.'

'Does it?' her husband replied. 'I wanted to keep a heart but I was worried about setting up one of dummy's black suits.'

His wife reached unsympathetically for her scorecard. 'I did bid hearts,' she said.

At half-time the monastery team was 25 IMPs in the lead, well on the way to the expected maximum 20-0 win in victory points. Two novices appeared in the cardroom, one bearing a large plate of jam sandwiches, the other a pot of tea.

Sheila Larkley inspected the refreshments with no great enthusiasm. 'I'm surprised you survive in these arctic conditions,' she observed. 'Can't you apply for a government grant or something? My mother had her loft insulated free of charge, just before she died. You should go down to the post office and ask them about it.'

The Abbot adopted a pious expression. 'Our physical comfort is of little concern to us,' he replied. 'We concentrate more on spiritual matters.'

Mrs Larkley was tempted to ask whether the physical comfort of his guests was of any concern. She would certainly wear more clothing if they ever had to play a winter match here again. Perhaps in future years they could stall throughout the cold season, claiming that someone was ill. Yes, they could delay the match until the Spring. She would suggest that to Bill and Dennis afterwards.

The Abbot returned to the playing room a few minutes before the others. He consulted his pocket thermometer, noting that the temperature was now down to 56. Excellent! The 20-0 win was as good as in the bag.

The second half saw the Abbot and Brother Xavier facing the Butterworths.

North-South game
Dealer South

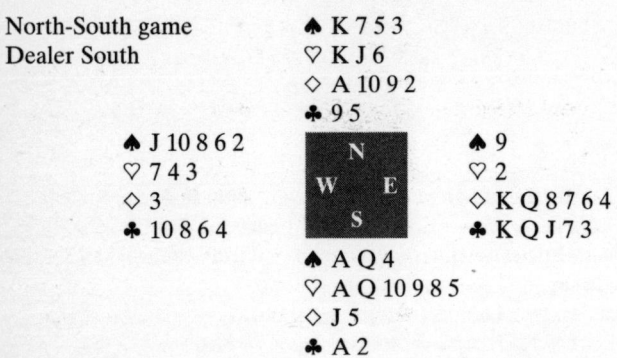

```
                 ♠ K 7 5 3
                 ♡ K J 6
                 ◇ A 10 9 2
                 ♣ 9 5
♠ J 10 8 6 2                      ♠ 9
♡ 7 4 3              N            ♡ 2
◇ 3             W       E         ◇ K Q 8 7 6 4
♣ 10 8 6 4          S            ♣ K Q J 7 3
                 ♠ A Q 4
                 ♡ A Q 10 9 8 5
                 ◇ J 5
                 ♣ A 2
```

WEST	NORTH	EAST	SOUTH
The	*Dennis*	*Brother*	*Evelyn*
Abbot	*Butterworth*	*Xavier*	*Butterworth*
–	–	–	1♡
Pass	1♠	2NT	4♡
Pass	4NT	Pass	5♠
Pass	6♡	All Pass	

The Abbot led his singleton diamond against the heart slam, wincing when the dummy went down. What appalling bidding! How could Blackwood be right with two top losers in clubs?

Evelyn Butterworth won the diamond lead with dummy's ace and drew two rounds of trumps with the king and ace. She then ran the jack of diamonds to East's queen. Brother Xavier paused to consider his return. If he simply knocked out declarer's ace of clubs, she would cross to the trump jack and take a ruffing finesse in diamonds, setting up a discard. The Abbot had indicated three trumps with a trump peter, so surely it must be better to return a low diamond. That would kill the discard on the diamond suit.

Evelyn Butterworth was not pleased to see the low diamond return. Resignedly she ruffed with one of her high trumps and drew the outstanding trump. The only hope now was that the spades would break 3-3, unlikely as this was after the 2NT overcall. Mind you, nothing could be lost by playing her last two trumps first. Perhaps the fat monk would throw his spade guard away. What a size he was! He was only a stone or two lighter than Dennis.

Mrs Butterworth followed her plan and soon arrived at this position:

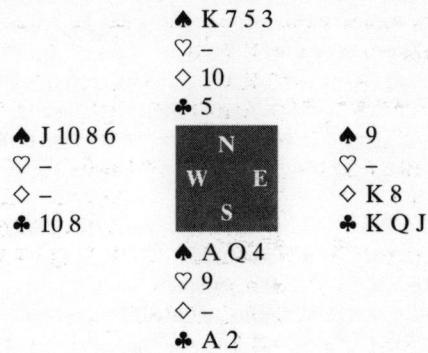

```
              ♠ K 7 5 3
              ♡ –
              ♦ 10
              ♣ 5
 ♠ J 10 8 6              ♠ 9
 ♡ –          N         ♡ –
 ♦ –        W   E       ♦ K 8
 ♣ 10 8       S         ♣ K Q J
              ♠ A Q 4
              ♡ 9
              ♦ –
              ♣ A 2
```

When the last heart was led, the Abbot threw another club. Evelyn Butterworth surveyed the scene with a helpless expression. It was obvious that West still had a spade guard. Prospects were surely non-existent unless . . . well, she would have to hope that East would discard the wrong thing. 'Throw a spade, please, Dennis,' she said.

Brother Xavier threw a diamond on declarer's last trump. Three rounds of spades, ending in the dummy, then squeezed him in the minors. He chose to retain the diamond king on the last spade and Mrs Butterworth scored the ace and two of clubs to make her slam.

'Well played indeed, Evelyn!' exclaimed Dennis Butterworth. 'It just shows how you mustn't give up at this game.'

Evelyn Butterworth was somewhat flushed by her success. 'I certainly didn't expect to make my two of clubs,' she replied.

The Abbot looked blackly across the table. 'Was it too difficult to play a club back?' he demanded. 'That breaks the squeeze.'

'Playing a club is no good,' Xavier replied. 'She can set up a diamond.'

Always an excuse, thought the Abbot. The secret of good defence was to concentrate 100% on the big deals. That's what he did himself and look at the result! When was the last time, if ever, that he had misdefended a big contract?

'You needed to ruff the second round of diamonds, Abbot,' said Brother Xavier. 'That kills the diamond discard and then you can switch to a club to break the squeeze.'

Would Brother Xavier never learn, thought the Abbot. Even if there was any sense in what he was saying, what was the point of mentioning double-dummy defences? Such observations could only improve the morale of the opponents, destroying all his good work with the heating system.

'Or you can lead a club, of course,' continued Brother Xavier.

'Ah yes, lead a club when I hold a singleton diamond,' replied the Abbot. 'I might also have stood on my head and spun round fifty times, singing the Hallelujah chorus.'

The monastery team won the match by just 17 IMPs, giving them a disappointing victory point score of 14-6. The visitors' departure was quickly executed, since they were already wearing their coats. After bidding them farewell, the Abbot turned sternly towards his team mates. 'Not the best of efforts,' he declared. 'I still don't understand how two of the world's worst overbidders failed to reach that heart slam in the second half.'

'We would bid it normally,' replied Brother Paulo. 'But the Unusual Notrump overcall suggested bad breaks.'

The Abbot rubbed the sleeves of his cassock, trying to restore the circulation to his arms. 'We need to warm up a bit in my study,' he said. 'I told one of the novices to keep a watchful eye on the fire. It should be quite cosy by now.'

'Does the heart slam make?' queried Brother Lucius, as the four monks climbed the stone staircase. 'How did the play go at your table?'

The Abbot was quick to get his response in first. 'The old dear stumbled into a non-simultaneous double squeeze,' he replied. 'She hadn't any idea what she was doing, but . . . playing against strong opposition, well, it seems to inspire some people!'

3.   Brother Aelred's Clever Rule

'Call me psychic but I think we'll get off to a good start this evening,' said the Abbot.

Brother Xavier delivered a cheerful smile. 'Why's that?' he asked. 'Are you feeling in good form?'

'Not particularly,' the Abbot replied. 'Brother Aelred is heading in this direction.'

Brother Aelred and his partner took their seats and the players drew their cards for the first board of the session:

East-West game
Dealer East

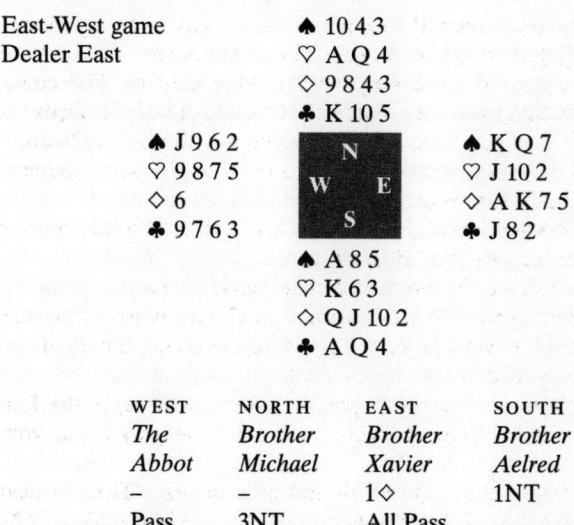

	♠ 10 4 3	
	♡ A Q 4	
	◇ 9 8 4 3	
	♣ K 10 5	
♠ J 9 6 2		♠ K Q 7
♡ 9 8 7 5		♡ J 10 2
◇ 6		◇ A K 7 5
♣ 9 7 6 3		♣ J 8 2
	♠ A 8 5	
	♡ K 6 3	
	◇ Q J 10 2	
	♣ A Q 4	

WEST	NORTH	EAST	SOUTH
The	*Brother*	*Brother*	*Brother*
Abbot	*Michael*	*Xavier*	*Aelred*
–	–	1◇	1NT
Pass	3NT	All Pass	

Sensing that declarer had the diamonds well held, the Abbot tried his luck in the spade suit. He led the two of spades and down went the dummy. 'Small, please,' said Brother Aelred.

The queen appeared from Brother Xavier, sitting East, and Brother Aelred surveyed the scene thoughtfully. He then paused to make some complex calculation, using the fingers of both hands. Nodding confidently as he digested the result, he played a low spade from his hand, allowing East's queen to win.

The Abbot raised his eyes to the ceiling. Since when was higher calculus required to hold up an ace in 3NT?

When the king of spades was returned, Brother Aelred resumed his calculations – once more making good use of his fingers.

The Abbot affected a look of disbelief. Brother Aelred normally played his cards with no thought at all. What on earth had caused this change of attitude? Not that any good would come from it, of course. A player of his standard would do better to play the card nearest his thumb.

His calculations complete, Brother Aelred won the second round of spades with the ace and led the ◇Q. Brother Xavier captured with the king and returned his last spade, allowing the Abbot to score two more tricks in the suit. The ace of diamonds was the defenders' fifth trick and the game went one down.

The Abbot's turned scornfully towards Brother Aelred. 'That's very nearly the worst piece of dummy play I've ever seen!' he exclaimed. 'Why on earth didn't you hold up the ace of spades for another round? That removes Xavier's last spade and you make the contract easily. You lose two diamonds and two spades.'

'That may be true as the cards lie,' replied Brother Aelred, 'but my play was absolutely correct, I assure you.'

The Abbot could not believe what he was hearing. Was the man ill?

Brother Aelred assumed a learned expression. 'I was applying the Rule of Seven,' he explained. 'An aunt of mine learnt it at her bridge classes and she wrote immediately to tell me about it. You add the number of cards in your own hand and the dummy, and then subtract the total from seven. The answer tells you how many rounds to hold up your ace – it's quite brilliant.'

'That's right, Abbot,' said Brother Michael. 'Did you follow that? Seven minus six is one, on this particular hand, so you hold up the ace for one round.'

'You're pulling my leg, surely?' said the Abbot. 'Hold up the ace twice and you remove Brother Xavier's spade holding, breaking our communications. That's the whole purpose of a hold-up!'

'The Abbot's right,' said Brother Xavier. 'Hold up twice and you make the contract easily.'

Brother Aelred shook his head. 'A Rule is a Rule,' he replied. 'My aunt says that all the strong players in New Malden are using it. With very good results, apparently.'

The Abbot could barely contain his exasperation. 'I've never heard such nonsense,' he declared. 'This Rule, as you call it, would give you the right answer if I happened to hold five spades. If I held four spades, or more than five spades, it would give you a completely wrong answer. What's more, on this deal you *knew* I had four spades because I led the two of the suit. You were absolutely certain to go down, the way you played it.'

Brother Aelred was unimpressed by this logic. 'Sometimes the best of plays go down,' he said. 'It doesn't mean they're wrong.'

'Quite right, partner,' said Brother Michael. 'Just because a finesse loses, it doesn't mean it was the wrong play.'

The Abbot decided it would be profitless to pursue the matter. Why would some players adopt any rule, however hopeless, rather than try to understand something? Anyone who understood that the purpose of a hold-up was to exhaust East's cards in the suit would make the contract easily. And what about those who purveyed this Rule of Seven? Had they not noticed that it failed whenever the lead was from a four-card suit? Had none of their students pointed this out to them? It was quite unbelievable.

Halfway through the evening, Lucius and Paulo arrived at the Abbot's table. This was the first board of the round:

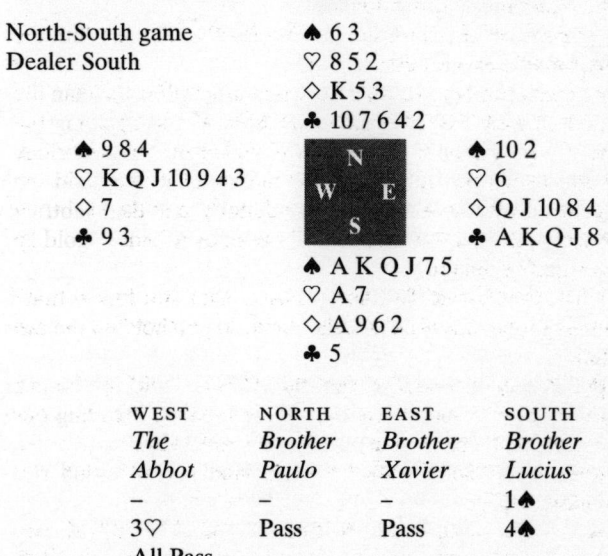

```
North-South game        ♠ 6 3
Dealer South            ♡ 8 5 2
                        ◇ K 5 3
                        ♣ 10 7 6 4 2
     ♠ 9 8 4                              ♠ 10 2
     ♡ K Q J 10 9 4 3          N          ♡ 6
     ◇ 7                    W     E        ◇ Q J 10 8 4
     ♣ 9 3                     S           ♣ A K Q J 8
                        ♠ A K Q J 7 5
                        ♡ A 7
                        ◇ A 9 6 2
                        ♣ 5
```

WEST	NORTH	EAST	SOUTH
The	*Brother*	*Brother*	*Brother*
Abbot	*Paulo*	*Xavier*	*Lucius*
–	–	–	1♠
3♡	Pass	Pass	4♠
All Pass			

Brother Lucius opened 1♠ and the Abbot could find no excuse to avoid making a weak jump overcall. His team mates had recently persuaded him to adopt this method, despite his decades-long opposition. When the overcall ran back to Brother Lucius, he closed the auction with a jump to the spade game.

The Abbot led the ♡K, won with the ace, and Lucius drew trumps in three rounds. There was no hurry to test the diamond position, so he played two further rounds of trumps instead. Brother Xavier, sitting East, chose a club and a diamond as his first two discards. He could not afford to throw a second diamond or declarer would play three rounds of the suit, setting up a long card in his hand. He therefore had to throw another club. Brother Lucius exited with a club, which East had to win, and these cards remained:

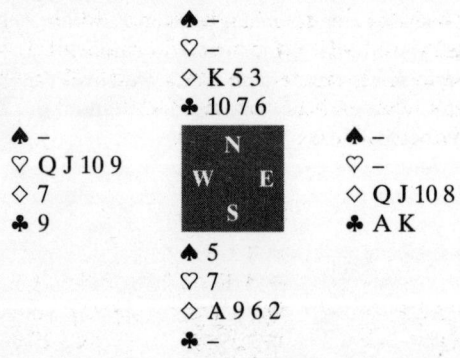

```
              ♠ –
              ♡ –
              ◇ K 5 3
              ♣ 10 7 6
♠ –                        ♠ –
♡ Q J 10 9                 ♡ –
◇ 7                        ◇ Q J 10 8
♣ 9                        ♣ A K
              ♠ 5
              ♡ 7
              ◇ A 9 6 2
              ♣ –
```

Brother Xavier, sitting East, paused to consider his defence. Since declarer had only one diamond entry to dummy, it was surely safe to play the ace of clubs. Lucius nodded to himself when this card appeared. After thinking for only a second or two, he allowed the club ace to win, discarding his last heart.

Brother Xavier could not afford to play his last top club, since this would establish a winner in dummy. He therefore switched to the queen of diamonds. This card, too, was allowed to win. It was the end of the road for the defence. East could still not afford to play his last club and therefore continued with the jack of diamonds. Brother Lucius won in the dummy, West showing out, and took the marked finesse of the nine of diamonds. The game had been made.

With a disgruntled air, the Abbot thrust his cards back into the wallet.

'Is something the matter, Abbot?' asked Brother Xavier.

'No, no, nothing at all,' the Abbot replied. 'I suppose it's a cold fact of life that Lucius always gets the chance to do something clever and we have to sit back and suffer the bottom.'

'I think we can all enjoy an attractive hand like that one,' said Brother Lucius. 'The result hardly matters at our stage of life.'

An amused Brother Paulo leaned forward. 'Perhaps you did have the chance to do something clever, Abbot,' he said. 'What about a club lead?'

'What on earth difference would that make?' grunted the Abbot. 'Not that any sane person would dream of leading a club when they had a solid heart sequence under their nose.'

'I needed my singleton club to throw Xavier on lead,' said Brother Lucius. 'There's no chance after a club lead.'

'It must be one of the Great Dealer's little jokes,' observed the Abbot. 'I've had three or four hands recently where leading from a sequence hasn't paid off. Of course, the moment I ignore a big sequence and look elsewhere, the other lead will cost and partner will say it was *obvious* to lead from the K-Q-J!'

This was the second deal of the round:

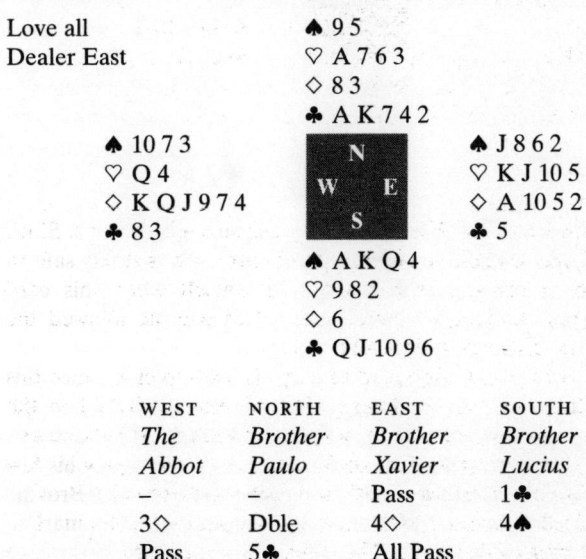

Love all
Dealer East

```
              ♠ 9 5
              ♡ A 7 6 3
              ◇ 8 3
              ♣ A K 7 4 2
♠ 10 7 3                        ♠ J 8 6 2
♡ Q 4          N                ♡ K J 10 5
◇ K Q J 9 7 4  W   E            ◇ A 10 5 2
♣ 8 3              S            ♣ 5
              ♠ A K Q 4
              ♡ 9 8 2
              ◇ 6
              ♣ Q J 10 9 6
```

WEST	NORTH	EAST	SOUTH
The	*Brother*	*Brother*	*Brother*
Abbot	*Paulo*	*Xavier*	*Lucius*
–	–	Pass	1♣
3◇	Dble	4◇	4♠
Pass	5♣	All Pass	

The Abbot groaned inwardly as he considered his opening lead. A black-suit lead was out of the question. Should he lead from his diamond sequence or make a wild stab with the queen of hearts? The other players would surely have a good laugh at his expense if a heart lead misfired. No, he must stick to his principles and lead the diamond king.

A low diamond was played from dummy and Brother Xavier paused to consider his play to the trick. On passive defence it was very likely that he would be squeezed in the major suits. If declarer's shape was 4-3-1-5, he would be able to ruff the second diamond, duck a heart and eventually squeeze him with dummy's last trump. Fortunately a remedy was at hand. He could overtake the diamond lead and play a spade. If declarer attempted to rectify the count by ducking a heart then, another round of spades would break the link between dummy and the South hand.

Brother Xavier produced the ace of diamonds at Trick 1 and unveiled his master plan, switching to a spade. Brother Lucius smiled at him. 'It seems that your turn has come to do something clever,' he said.

Xavier smiled back. 'We do our best,' he said.

Lucius won with the ace of spades and drew trumps in two rounds. He then ruffed a diamond in the South hand and proceeded to run dummy's trumps. This end position arose:

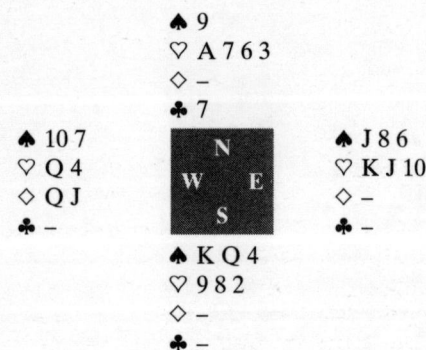

♠ 9
♡ A 7 6 3
◇ —
♣ 7

♠ 10 7
♡ Q 4
◇ Q J
♣ —

♠ J 8 6
♡ K J 10
◇ —
♣ —

♠ K Q 4
♡ 9 8 2
◇ —
♣ —

'Play the last trump,' said Brother Lucius.

Brother Xavier, sitting East, knew from South's bid in spades that he could not afford to discard a spade. Hoping for the best, he threw the ♡10. Leading a low heart from dummy would not be good enough for declarer at this stage. West would be able to win with the heart queen and cash his two good diamonds. Brother Lucius therefore crossed to the king of spades and led the ♡9 from his hand. The Abbot attempted to stop the card being run into the safe East hand by covering with the queen. 'Win with the ace,' said Brother Lucius.

When a second round of hearts was led, it was East who had to win the trick. Lucius, meanwhile, was careful to unblock the ♡8. With only spades in his hand, East had to lead a spade to South's queen and

Lucius could now lead the ♡2, claiming dummy's two hearts for the contract.

Brother Paulo's eyes lit up. 'Well played indeed, partner!' he exclaimed. 'Anyone would think these hands had been specially set.'

'Another bad one for the lead from a sequence, Abbot,' said Brother Xavier. 'A heart lead gives him no chance.'

'If a doubleton queen is the sort of opening lead you want, you should partner the village idiot instead of me,' declared the Abbot. 'Have you never studied the Table of Good Leads?'

'A spade lead beats it too,' said Brother Lucius. 'When I duck a trick in one of the red suits, you can play another spade and kill the link to my hand.'

Brother Xavier managed to keep a straight face. 'It's so true what you were telling Brother Aelred, Abbot,' he said. 'These rules, such as "always lead from a K-Q-J" . . . they're very overrated!'

4.   The Abbot's Olympic Dreams

'I found it most uplifting, the English team's success in the Olympiad,' said Brother Lucius, taking his seat.

'I can't say I was particularly impressed,' replied the Abbot. 'Most of the other countries are fairly weak. I expect we would have done quite well ourselves.' He turned towards the Italian monk, Brother Paulo. 'England lost to your lot by a huge margin, didn't they?'

'Yes, but that was in the semi-finals,' continued Brother Lucius. 'If I remember rightly, you didn't think England would even qualify for the knock-out stages.'

'I don't rate that bearded guy, David Burn, very highly,' declared the Abbot. 'I once made 3NT doubled against him at Brighton.'

Brother Xavier laughed. 'I remember, Abbot,' he said. 'But that was over twenty years ago. He was only a junior, wasn't he?'

'Even so, a club switch was obvious,' replied the Abbot. 'Any true bridge player would have found it.'

The monks drew their cards for this board:

```
Love all                   ♠ K 8 6
Dealer West                ♡ A 7 3 2
                           ◇ A 8 6
                           ♣ A J 7
        ♠ –                              ♠ Q J 4
        ♡ K Q J 9 6 4         N          ♡ 8 5
        ◇ 9 4 3          W        E      ◇ K 10 7 2
        ♣ 9 5 3 2            S          ♣ Q 10 8 4
                           ♠ A 10 9 7 5 3 2
                           ♡ 10
                           ◇ Q J 5
                           ♣ K 6
```

WEST	NORTH	EAST	SOUTH
Brother	*Brother*	*Brother*	*The*
Paulo	*Xavier*	*Lucius*	*Abbot*
2♡	2NT	Pass	5♠
Pass	6♠	All Pass	

A somewhat rustic sequence carried the Abbot to a small slam and the ♡K was led. 'Plenty of top cards for you,' observed Brother Xavier as he put down the dummy. 'Not much shape, though.'

The Abbot nodded happily as he surveyed the dummy. An excellent slam bid on just 26 points! Not many teams would have reached it in the Olympiad. The Italians and the Americans maybe. Burn and Callaghan would have stopped in game, you can be sure. 'Ace, please,' he said.

The Abbot crossed to the ace of trumps and could not believe his luck when West showed out. It just went to prove his point. The English North-South pair would have stopped in game and picked up a big swing when the trumps were 3-0. Anyone could get through to a semi-final if luck was blowing so powerfully in their direction.

The Abbot returned to dummy with the king of trumps and ruffed a heart, to remove East's last card in the suit. He then threw East on lead with a trump. Brother Lucius, sitting East, had to find an exit in this position:

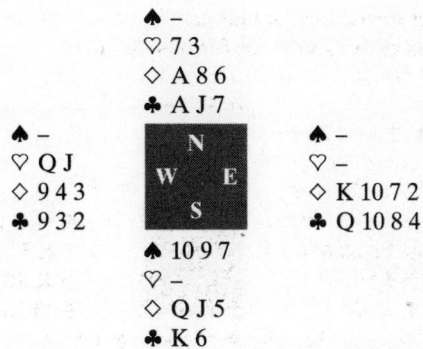

```
              ♠ –
              ♡ 7 3
              ◇ A 8 6
              ♣ A J 7
♠ –           ┌─────────┐        ♠ –
♡ Q J         │    N    │        ♡ –
◇ 9 4 3       │ W     E │        ◇ K 10 7 2
♣ 9 3 2       │    S    │        ♣ Q 10 8 4
              └─────────┘
              ♠ 10 9 7
              ♡ –
              ◇ Q J 5
              ♣ K 6
```

South was marked with the ♣K, so a club switch into the tenace would clearly cost a trick. Many defenders would have switched to a low diamond by now but Brother Lucius paused to count how many tricks declarer would have after a club switch – six spades, one heart, one diamond and three clubs. Only eleven!

Since prospects were somewhat unknown on a diamond switch, Brother Lucius placed a small club on the table. The Abbot scored three tricks in the club suit, throwing a diamond, but then had to take the diamond finesse. When it failed, he was one down.

'Excellent defence, partner!' exclaimed Brother Paulo. 'If you play a diamond, the Abbot wins the queen, cashes the diamond ace and runs the trumps. You are squeezed in the minors.'

'That's certainly what I had in mind,' declared the Abbot. 'Had there been any justice, the trumps would have broken 2-1.'

A round or two later, two novices arrived at the Abbot's table.

'Good evening, Abbot,' said Brother Mark. 'Excellent news about England reaching the semi-final in the Olympiad, wasn't it?'

'Did they?' said the Abbot. 'I hear the standard wasn't very good this year.'

'They beat Norway, Helgemo's team, in the quarter-finals,' said Brother Adam. 'I was reading about an excellent 3NT that Glyn Liggins made against them.'

'Liggins? He's editor of *BRIDGE Magazine*, isn't he?' grunted the Abbot. 'If he was any good at playing the game he would concentrate on that, rather than just writing about it.'

'That Horton character is editor now,' said Brother Xavier.

'It makes no difference,' declared the Abbot. 'No one who writes about the game has the first idea how to play it, believe me.'

This was the first board of the round:

East-West game
Dealer South

```
              ♠ J 10
              ♡ Q J 9 8 5 3
              ◇ J 6 3
              ♣ Q 5
  ♠ A K 6 4          N          ♠ 9 7 5 3
  ♡ 7 4                          ♡ 10 6 2
  ◇ 9         W         E        ◇ A K 10 5 4
  ♣ J 10 9 6 3 2       S        ♣ 8
              ♠ Q 8 2
              ♡ A K
              ◇ Q 8 7 2
              ♣ A K 7 4
```

WEST	NORTH	EAST	SOUTH
The	*Brother*	*Brother*	*Brother*
Abbot	*Mark*	*Xavier*	*Adam*
–	–	–	1◇
Pass	1♡	Pass	2NT
Pass	3NT	All Pass	

The Abbot led the jack of clubs and down went the dummy. Brother Adam nodded thoughtfully as he surveyed its contents. There were nine tricks available in hearts and clubs. Unfortunately, the club lead had introduced a blockage in the suit.

He won the club lead with the ace and cashed the two top hearts. A club to dummy's queen was followed by the remaining cards in dummy's heart suit. These cards were left in play:

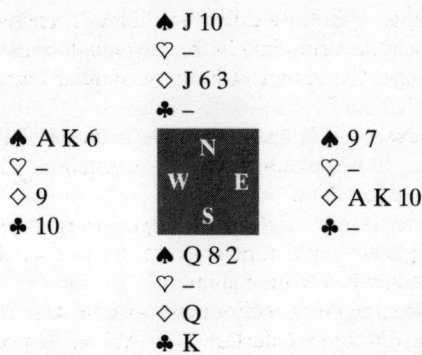

```
                    ♠ J 10
                    ♡ –
                    ◇ J 6 3
                    ♣ –
      ♠ A K 6         N          ♠ 9 7
      ♡ –                        ♡ –
      ◇ 9        W       E       ◇ A K 10
      ♣ 10           S           ♣ –
                    ♠ Q 8 2
                    ♡ –
                    ◇ Q
                    ♣ K
```

When Brother Adam called for the jack of spades, Brother Xavier signalled his count with the nine. It was not difficult for the Abbot to read the position. He won with the king and returned the nine of diamonds. Xavier cashed his two top diamonds and declarer had no card to spare. Whether he threw a spade or a club, the Abbot would have the remaining tricks. The game was one down.

'Oh dear, oh dear!' exclaimed the Abbot, turning towards the young declarer. 'Wasn't it obvious that was going to happen?'

'My club winners were blocked, Abbot,' the novice replied. 'It was rather awkward.'

'Play the two top hearts, then a spade,' continued the Abbot. 'That's what you should have done. Even if I return a club, you still make it. When you eventually come off dummy with a second spade, there's no link card for the defensive squeeze.'

Brother Adam could not follow a word of this. 'Yes, I see,' he replied. 'That's a very clever analysis, Abbot.'

The Abbot nodded happily. Just imagine how the Olympiad Vu-Graph audience would have enjoyed a defence like that. The commentators would have been lost for words.

'It's a complete top for us,' announced Brother Mark, inspecting the scoresheet. 'Everyone else has gone two down in Four Hearts.'

'Yes, it was an inspired 3NT bid,' said Brother Xavier. 'Against a heart contract we can take two ace-kings and a diamond ruff.'

The Abbot sat back in his chair. A brilliantly timed defensive squeeze that would have made the front page of the Olympiad Bulletin . . . and it hadn't brought him a single match-point.

The Abbot's mood was not improved by the arrival, a round later, of his least favourite opponent.

'Did you hear about that 1◇ opening by Gunnar Hallberg against Italy, Abbot?' asked Brother Cameron, sinking heavily into the South seat. 'Two small diamonds, he had, and five good spades!'

Brother Damien laughed. 'Simpson responded 1♡ and the Italian had no available bid on a hand with six diamonds to the A-K-Q-J. His partner led a club against 3NT and that was 12 IMPs in!'

'How do you know about these deals?' demanded the Abbot. 'The magazines covering the event can't possibly be out yet.'

'It's all on the Internet,' Brother Cameron replied. 'You can play through all the hands on VuGraph.'

The Abbot's mouth fell open. 'I installed the Internet for the express purpose of gathering charitable donations,' he declared. 'They charge an arm and a leg for connection time. You can't waste valuable monastery resources, watching players make irresponsible bids on a small doubleton!'

A strained silence reigned as the players sorted their cards for the first board of the round:

North-South game	♠ A K
Dealer West	♡ A
	◇ A K Q 8 6 5 2
	♣ K 5 4

♠ Q	N	♠ 9 7 4
♡ K J 9 7 4 2	W E	♡ Q 10 6
◇ J 9 7 4	S	◇ 10
♣ J 7		♣ A Q 10 9 8 3

	♠ J 10 8 6 5 3 2
	♡ 8 5 3
	◇ 3
	♣ 6 2

WEST	NORTH	EAST	SOUTH
The	*Brother*	*Brother*	*Brother*
Abbot	*Damien*	*Xavier*	*Cameron*
2♡	Double	4♡	4♠
Pass	6◇	Pass	6♠
All Pass			

The Abbot led the ♡7 against the spade slam, dummy's ace winning the trick. Brother Cameron paused for thought. If trumps were 2-2 and diamonds 3-2, there would be no problem. He could simply draw trumps and cash a bundle of winners, making an overtrick. What if the diamonds divided 4-1? It seemed that he had nothing to lose by cashing the ◇A and ruffing a diamond. If the second round was overruffed, the other line would have failed too.

Brother Cameron cashed the ◇A and called for a low diamond, ruffing low when Brother Xavier threw a club. When a trump was played to dummy's ace, the queen appeared from the Abbot. Reading this as a singleton, Brother Cameron continued with a high diamond from dummy. Brother Xavier could see that it would be hopeless to ruff. Even if declarer held only six trumps, he could overruff and cross to dummy's trump king, drawing the adverse trumps. Brother Xavier discarded on the third and fourth diamonds, hoping that the Abbot held another trump and could deal with the fifth diamond. It was not to be. Brother Cameron continued to throw losers from his hand and made all thirteen tricks.

The Abbot turned aghast towards the young declarer. 'That line of play was way against the odds!' he exclaimed. 'Any top-class defender would false-card the queen of trumps from queen doubleton. A doubleton queen is three times as likely as a singleton queen.'

Brother Cameron looked back impassively. The Abbot was right. Playing against someone capable of such a false card, it would be right to play for a 2-2 trump break.

'We needed a club lead, Abbot,' said Brother Xavier. 'Four Clubs was my bid, playing fit-jumps, and then you'd have led a club. You don't like to play them, of course.'

'There was a good fit-jump hand in the England-Belgium match,' said Brother Cameron. 'Fawcett held five spades to the . . .'

'That's quite enough of that,' declared the Abbot. 'Second-rate players may need to prop themselves up with such artificialities, but not me. I've done well enough without them for forty years.'

The last round brought two of the monastery's lesser lights to the Abbot's table, Brother Martin and his rotund partner, Brother Hubert.

'Hullo, Abbot,' said Brother Hubert, easing himself into the West seat. 'Wasn't it a wonderful sunny day?'

The Abbot gave a small sigh of relief. What a joy it was to be facing opponents who probably didn't even know that the Olympiad had taken place. Two easy tops against them and his mood would be very nearly back to normal.

'It's amazing how well England did in the Olympiad,' continued Brother Hubert. 'That young Brother Cameron has been printing down the Bulletin from the Internet. He delivers my copy at seven o'clock every morning. Nice young lad.'

'He brings me one, too,' said Brother Martin. 'It's very much appreciated, I can tell you.'

The Abbot shook his head in disbelief. Did Brother Cameron not realise the cost of ink-jet cartridges? And why had no copy of the Bulletin arrived under his own cell door?

The last round began with this board:

East-West game
Dealer South

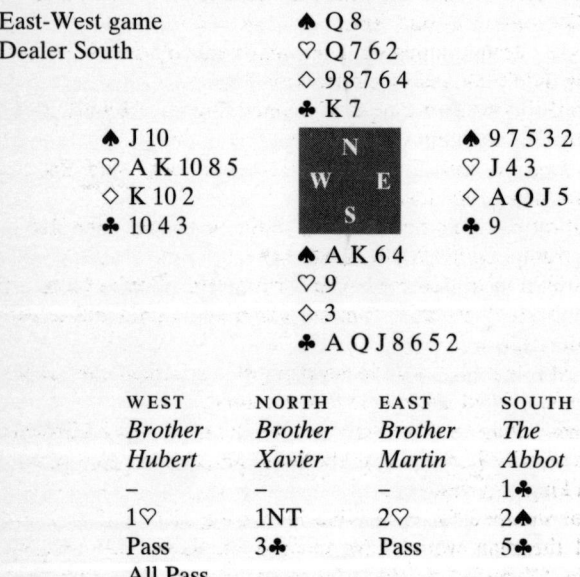

```
                    ♠ Q 8
                    ♡ Q 7 6 2
                    ◇ 9 8 7 6 4
                    ♣ K 7
  ♠ J 10                         ♠ 9 7 5 3 2
  ♡ A K 10 8 5       N           ♡ J 4 3
  ◇ K 10 2        W     E        ◇ A Q J 5
  ♣ 10 4 3          S            ♣ 9
                    ♠ A K 6 4
                    ♡ 9
                    ◇ 3
                    ♣ A Q J 8 6 5 2
```

WEST	NORTH	EAST	SOUTH
Brother	*Brother*	*Brother*	*The*
Hubert	*Xavier*	*Martin*	*Abbot*
–	–	–	1♣
1♡	1NT	2♡	2♠
Pass	3♣	Pass	5♣
All Pass			

Brother Hubert spent quite a while deciding on his lead, pulling out one card then pushing it back. No-one in the bridge universe was more often 'in doubt' about the best opening lead and it was no surprise when he eventually placed a trump on the table.

The Abbot won the trump lead with the jack and then cashed the queen and ace of spades successfully. If spades had started 4-3 it would suit his purposes to play the king of spades before ruffing the fourth round of the suit. If instead he ruffed the third round, he might suffer a spade ruff when he came off the dummy. West's ten and jack of spades rather suggested that spades were 2-5, however, and the Abbot decided to lead his low spade next. A heart discard appeared from West and he ruffed with the bare king of trumps in dummy.

'Small heart,' said the Abbot, hoping for the best.

The Abbot was pleased to see a small spot-card appear from East. He covered with the nine and West won with the ten. The Abbot muttered a small prayer, hoping that West would hold the $\diamond$A. Surely, if that were the case, a player such as Brother Hubert would not be capable of an underlead to partner's king.

The prayer did not reach its destination. Knowing from the bidding that declarer had no more hearts, Brother Hubert switched to a low diamond. Brother Martin won with the ace and gave his partner a spade ruff. The game was one down.

'That was a strange opening lead, partner,' observed Brother Martin. 'Why didn't you lead your ace-king?'

'It may work better as it happens,' replied Brother Hubert, 'but I was put off by the no-trump bid over me.'

'A trump was the only lead to beat the contract,' said Brother Xavier. 'It was a very fine lead.'

The Abbot returned his cards wearily to the board. Brother Hubert always led a trump. Didn't Xavier realise that?

Brother Hubert inspected the North curtain card. 'You're better off in 3NT, aren't you?' he said. 'I'm surprised you didn't bid it with queen-to-four sitting over me.'

'You take the first six tricks in no-trumps!' exclaimed the Abbot. 'You win the heart lead and switch to a diamond.'

'A diamond switch would be very double-dummy,' replied Brother Hubert. 'It's usually best to clear the long suit. I don't like playing away from a king, anyway.'

The Abbot slumped forward. Nine black-suit tricks visible in the dummy and the man would have cleared the heart suit! Perhaps success in the Olympiad wouldn't be so easy to achieve after all. It wasn't enough to bid to superb contracts like this Five Clubs. With his luck, opponents such as Martinique and Botswana would put their thumb on a trump lead, at just the right moment for them.

With a resigned air the Abbot sat back in his chair. No, it had been fair enough to give the younger generation a chance in the English team. Even if they did lose heavily to Italy.

5.   Josie Threlfall's Valuable Advice

'There was a phone call while you were out, Abbot,' said Brother Lucius. 'William Threlfall has had to go into hospital suddenly, for a hernia operation. He won't be able to play tonight.'

'That's all we needed!' exclaimed the Abbot. 'It took me ages to arrange this match and we're right at the end of the period. No chance of him delaying the operation until tomorrow, I suppose?'

'The match is still on, actually,' said Brother Lucius. 'His wife will be taking his place.'

The Abbot looked as if he had just won the national lottery. 'His wife, did you say?' he exclaimed. 'She's absolutely hopeless. Runs some beginners' class in Lyndhurst, doesn't she? I'm surprised she doesn't attend the class, rather than run it. Well, the match should be an absolute walk-over for us now.'

At seven o'clock in George Barr's cottage in Micheldever the first-round county knock-out match began. This was an early board:

East-West game
Dealer South

```
                    ♠ 8 5 2
                    ♡ A J 5 3
                    ◇ A 9 6
                    ♣ J 6 4
   ♠ 10 3                          ♠ 6 4
   ♡ 9              N              ♡ Q 10 8 6
   ◇ K Q J 10 4 2  W   E          ◇ 8 5 3
   ♣ A 10 5 2          S          ♣ K Q 9 7
                    ♠ A K Q J 9 7
                    ♡ K 7 4 2
                    ◇ 7
                    ♣ 8 3
```

WEST	NORTH	EAST	SOUTH
The	*Josie*	*Brother*	*George*
Abbot	*Threlfall*	*Xavier*	*Barr*
–	–	–	1♠
2◇	2♠	Pass	4♠
All Pass			

The Abbot led the ◇K and Josie Threlfall laid out her dummy. 'I hope this is all right,' she said. 'Bill likes me to raise him on three trumps. I forgot to ask you if you prefer three or four trumps.'

'It's fine, Josie,' said the white-haired George Barr. 'Win with the ace, will you?'

After ruffing a diamond in the South hand, declarer drew trumps in two rounds. He then crossed to the ♡A and ruffed dummy's last diamond. His preparations at an end, he exited with a club.

The Abbot and Brother Xavier had no alternative but to win the first two rounds of clubs and continue the suit. George Barr ruffed the third round and surveyed this end position:

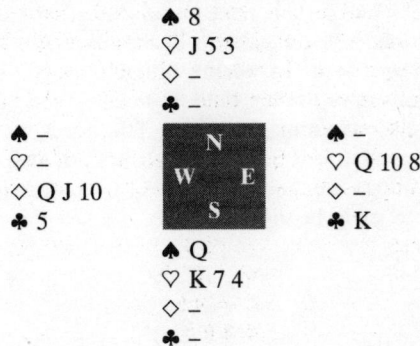

```
                    ♠ 8
                    ♡ J 5 3
                    ◇ -
                    ♣ -
    ♠ -                          ♠ -
    ♡ -          N               ♡ Q 10 8
    ◇ Q J 10   W   E             ◇ -
    ♣ 5          S               ♣ K
                    ♠ Q
                    ♡ K 7 4
                    ◇ -
                    ♣ -
```

When a low heart was led towards the dummy, the Abbot showed out and Mrs Thelfall reached for the jack. 'No, no, play a small heart,' instructed the declarer.

Brother Xavier won the eight of hearts and was end-played. 'You played it well,' he said, smiling at declarer. 'What poison shall I choose? I think I'll play the club.'

George Barr threw a heart from his hand and ruffed in the dummy. Ten tricks were his.

'Difficult for you, Abbot,' said Brother Xavier. 'If you happen to lead your singleton heart, I don't think he can do it. He needed the ace of hearts as an entry.'

Josie Threlfall gave the Abbot a friendly smile. 'It's amazing how often a singleton lead works out well,' she observed. 'If partner has the ace he can give you a ruff.'

For a brief moment the Abbot closed his eyes. If she was going to deliver a Lyndhurst Beginner's Tip at the end of every hand, the match would prove quite an ordeal.

Meanwhile, in the somewhat under-sized kitchen, Lucius and Paulo faced James Glasson and Hugh Burnett. Despite the powerful central-heating, both were well wrapped up. Hugh Burnett had a thick woollen scarf coiled round his neck.

Brother Lucius had just picked up this hand:

♠ Q J 2
♡ A 3
♢ A K 8 6
♣ A 9 8 6

There was a pre-emptive opening of Three Hearts on his right and he doubled for take-out. The next player passed and Brother Paulo jumped to Six Spades. Lucius thumbed through his cards, a smile on his lips. Facing 99.5% of the world's bridge players, his hand represented an obvious raise to the grand. It so happened that his present partner belonged to the remaining 0.5%. Still, surely he couldn't hold less than seven spades to the A-K and a side king, or six good spades and a couple of minor-suit honours. Brother Lucius raised to the grand slam and this proved to be the full deal:

Love all
Dealer West

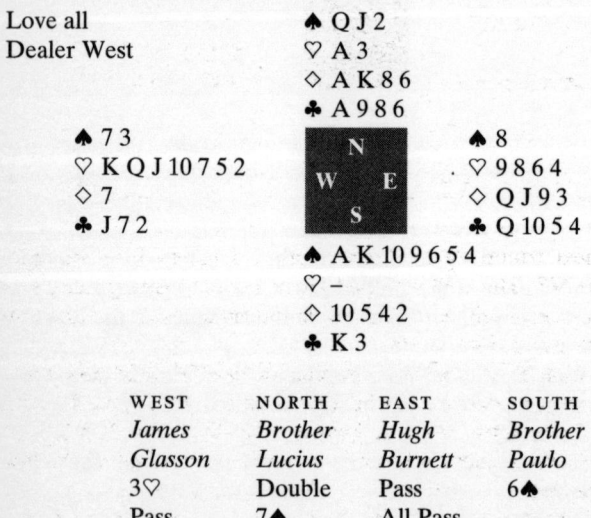

♠ Q J 2
♡ A 3
♢ A K 8 6
♣ A 9 8 6

♠ 7 3
♡ K Q J 10 7 5 2
♢ 7
♣ J 7 2

♠ 8
♡ 9 8 6 4
♢ Q J 9 3
♣ Q 10 5 4

♠ A K 10 9 6 5 4
♡ –
♢ 10 5 4 2
♣ K 3

WEST	NORTH	EAST	SOUTH
James	Brother	Hugh	Brother
Glasson	Lucius	Burnett	Paulo
3♡	Double	Pass	6♠
Pass	7♠	All Pass	

Brother Paulo won the heart lead with dummy's ace and discarded a diamond. He then drew trumps in two rounds, East throwing a heart.

What were the prospects? West appeared to hold nine cards in the majors, leaving only four cards in the minors. If he had two clubs and two diamonds, declarer could cash the diamond ace-king and run his trumps, catching East in a simple squeeze.

With seven clubs out and only five diamonds, it was perhaps more likely that West held three clubs and one diamond. What could be done in that case? Isolating the club guard was no good because East would be discarding after the dummy. No, he would have to play for a trump squeeze, keeping the club holding intact and throwing two diamonds from the dummy. The snag with a trump squeeze was that some guesswork might be involved at the key moment. Ah well, thought Brother Paulo, let's run the trump suit and see what happens.

On the next two trumps East discarded one more heart and then a diamond. Brother Paulo threw a diamond from dummy, leaving these cards still to be played:

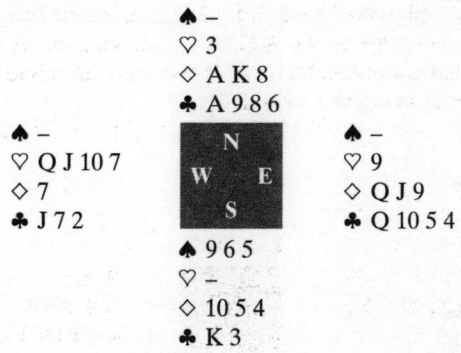

On the next trump Paulo threw another diamond from dummy, retaining the ♡3. The well-wrapped Hugh Burnett, sitting East, was reluctant to weaken either of his minor-suit holdings. He eventually decided to throw his last heart.

This was what Paulo had been hoping to see. He could now wave goodbye to any guesswork in the end position. West guarded the hearts and East almost certainly guarded the diamonds. It followed that neither defender would be able to guard the clubs when the last trump was played.

Brother Paulo cashed the two top diamonds in dummy, West showing out on the second round. He then returned to the king of clubs and played his last two trumps. As he had foreseen, a classic double squeeze arose. Neither defender was able to retain a club guard and thirteen tricks were made.

'Why did it take you so long to raise to the grand?' queried Paulo, chuckling to himself. 'You do not trust my bidding?'

'I'd have felt happier with another ace in my hand,' Brother Lucius replied.

The first half was nearing its conclusion when the Abbot picked up this hand:

> ♠ 4
> ♡ K 10 5 2
> ♢ 10 8 4 2
> ♣ K 9 8 5

George Barr, on his right, opened One Spade and was raised to Four Spades. There was no further bidding and the Abbot had to find a lead. What was best? Only the feeble-minded would lead a singleton trump. Nor was a diamond in the least bit attractive. It had to be a heart or a club and the presence of the ten made a heart the more attractive proposition.

The Abbot led the ♡2 and this proved to be the whole deal:

Game all
Dealer South

	♠ A K J 9 2	
	♡ 8 6 3	
	♢ A J	
	♣ A 7 2	

♠ 4		♠ 8 6
♡ K 10 5 2	N	♡ Q 9 7
♢ 10 8 4 2	W E	♢ Q 9 7 6 3
♣ K 9 8 5	S	♣ J 10 3

	♠ Q 10 7 5 3	
	♡ A J 4	
	♢ K 5	
	♣ Q 6 4	

WEST	NORTH	EAST	SOUTH
The	*Josie*	*Brother*	*George*
Abbot	*Threlfall*	*Xavier*	*Barr*
–	–	–	1♠
Pass	4♠	All Pass	

The Abbot could not believe the riches laid out in the dummy. Was this the sort of raise of One Spade to Four Spades that was recommended to the beginners of Lyndhurst? It was truly amazing that such hopeless players should want to teach the game. It would be no more than justice if they had missed a cold slam.

'Thank you, Josie,' said George Barr. 'This could be a tricky one.'

The Abbot closed his eyes, as if in pain. Tricky one, with a dummy like that? It was absolutely typical of his luck that declarer should hold a storming minimum when the dummy had underbid by three tricks.

Barr won East's queen of hearts with the ace and drew trumps in two rounds. He then played two rounds of diamonds, removing that suit from the scene. The lead was in dummy and these cards remained:

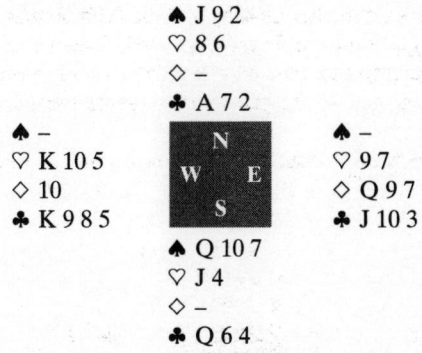

```
              ♠ J 9 2
              ♡ 8 6
              ◇ –
              ♣ A 7 2
  ♠ –                        ♠ –
  ♡ K 10 5                   ♡ 9 7
  ◇ 10                       ◇ Q 9 7
  ♣ K 9 8 5                  ♣ J 10 3
              ♠ Q 10 7
              ♡ J 4
              ◇ –
              ♣ Q 6 4
```

The ♡6 was led from the dummy and East covered with the seven. George Barr turned towards Brother Xavier. 'Does your partner's lead of the two of hearts promise an honour?' he queried.

'If the lead is from length, yes, he would normally hold an honour,' Xavier replied. 'We lead second-best from bad suits. The only other possibility is a singleton.'

'I thought your partner didn't like leading singletons,' persisted George Barr.

Brother Xavier smiled politely. 'Those are our methods, anyway,' he said.

Deciding that West was a strong favourite to hold the king of hearts, declarer played low on the second round of hearts. Brother Xavier's ♡7 held the trick and he switched to the jack of clubs. Realising that it would be premature to try the queen at this stage, Barr won the trick with dummy's ace of clubs. He then exited with a third round of hearts. The Abbot won with the king and had no option but to lead from his king of clubs. The game had been made.

'Oh, well played, George!' exclaimed Josie Threlfall. 'That was what they call a throw-in play, wasn't it?'

'That's right,' her partner replied. 'I was a bit lucky with the opening lead. I don't think I can make it if this gentleman leads a diamond or a trump.'

'May I?' said Josie Threlfall, retrieving the Abbot's cards from the table. Somewhat painstakingly, she sorted them into suits. 'It just shows how dangerous it is to lead from a king,' she said. 'I always warn my pupils against it. You don't mind if I write this hand down, do you? It will be such an instructive example for them.'

With some difficulty the Abbot suppressed an urge to throttle the woman. Was she not aware that he had played the game at the very highest level for four decades?

'It's a close decision whether a trump or a diamond is the best lead,' Josie Threlfall continued. 'If I set it as a test, I think I'll have to give both those leads full marks.'

6.   The Abbot's Magnificent Recovery

The monastery team was 12 IMPs adrift at half-time in the local knock-out match against moderate opposition from Lyndhurst.

'I thought it would be nearer 30 IMPs,' said Josie Threlfall, passing a plate of sardine sandwiches in the Abbot's direction. 'I had four big ticks on our scorecard against you.'

The Abbot waved the proffered plate aside – sardines were not a favourite of his – and reached instead for a slice of walnut cake. 'It's a difficult business, assessing the boards,' he replied. 'I had our team well ahead on my card.'

The second half began with the Abbot and Brother Xavier facing the two elderly men, James Glasson and Hugh Burnett.

This was the first board they played:

Game all
Dealer North

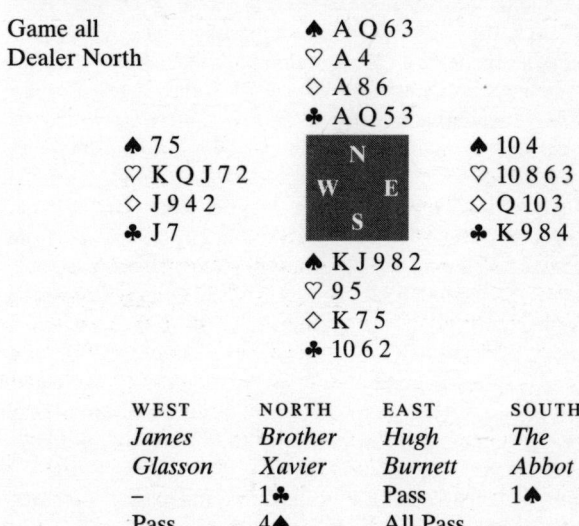

	♠ A Q 6 3	
	♡ A 4	
	◇ A 8 6	
	♣ A Q 5 3	

♠ 7 5	♠ 10 4
♡ K Q J 7 2	♡ 10 8 6 3
◇ J 9 4 2	◇ Q 10 3
♣ J 7	♣ K 9 8 4

| |
| ♠ K J 9 8 2 |
| ♡ 9 5 |
| ◇ K 7 5 |
| ♣ 10 6 2 |

WEST	NORTH	EAST	SOUTH
James	*Brother*	*Hugh*	*The*
Glasson	*Xavier*	*Burnett*	*Abbot*
–	1♣	Pass	1♠
Pass	4♠	All Pass	

Rating his hand too thin for 2NT, Brother Xavier opened proceedings at the one level. The Abbot was soon in a spade game and West led the king of hearts.

James Glasson gave the Abbot a friendly smile as the dummy went down. 'There shouldn't be any problem with a dummy like that,' he observed.

'Play the ace,' said the Abbot. After drawing trumps with the ace and king, he turned his mind to the club suit. Two tricks from the suit would give him the game. How about cashing the ace of clubs and then playing low to the ten? Yes, it seemed that would fail only when West held precisely jack doubleton in the suit. It was very nearly a 100% line.

'Ace of clubs,' said the Abbot, in a masterful tone.

Hugh Burnett peered out from above his thick scarf. 'You're in your hand, I think,' he said.

The Abbot could not stand opponents who were so pedantic on the mechanics of the game. What on earth did it matter which hand he was in when he was cashing an ace? Did the man think he was void in the suit?

No cards of interest fell under the club ace and the Abbot continued with a club to the ten, not overjoyed to see this losing to the jack. West cashed a heart trick and then switched to a diamond. The Abbot won with the diamond king and led a third round of clubs towards dummy. He could not believe it when West showed out, discarding a heart. There was no way to avoid a subsequent diamond loser and the game went one down.

'How amazing!' James Glasson exclaimed. 'With so many points in the dummy, I'd have bet anything that you would make that.'

The Abbot glared blackly at his opponent. Rudeness from a certain uncultured member of the novitiate he was accustomed to. Rudeness from someone who'd been granted over seven decades to acquire good manners, well, there was no excuse for it.

'What happens if you exit with a heart after drawing trumps?' asked Brother Xavier. 'Is that any good?'

The Abbot sighed patiently. Was he surrounded by idiots? 'They win and knock out one of my diamond stoppers,' he replied. 'I'd have no chance of setting up a club discard then.'

'No, but can't you take your two diamonds and play a diamond back?' continued Brother Xavier. 'They would have to open the clubs for you. Both the red suits would be eliminated.'

The Abbot could not believe what he was hearing. Was Xavier determined to raise the morale of these hopeless opponents? His suggestion made little sense anyway. If he gave up a heart after drawing trumps, West would be able to attack clubs from his side of the table. That would break up the endplay when East held the king and jack. It was typical of Xavier to analyse on a double-dummy basis.

'I think that line's safe against any lie of the cards,' said Brother

Xavier. 'West can't attack clubs when East holds both the honours, or you can set up a club trick for a diamond discard.'

The Abbot closed his eyes for a second, realising that he had misplayed the hand. 'I think we've all got the point by now,' he declared. 'You should have opened One Spade or a sensible 2NT. Then you could have played it yourself, rather than wasting so much time criticising my play.'

Glasson and Burnett shared a surprised glance. George had warned them of the Abbot's reputation for rudeness. Still, they hadn't expected anything like this – not from a man of the cloth.

Back in the cramped kitchen, Lucius and Paulo faced Josie Threlfall and George Barr.

East-West game
Dealer South

```
                      ♠ 9 8
                      ♡ A K 5 2
                      ◇ 9 7 3
                      ♣ Q 8 7 5
   ♠ A K Q 10 4                      ♠ 6 5 3 2
   ♡ Q 7 6 3          N              ♡ 10 9
   ◇ 10 4 2       W       E          ◇ Q 8 6
   ♣ 2                S              ♣ J 9 4 3
                      ♠ J 7
                      ♡ J 8 4
                      ◇ A K J 5
                      ♣ A K 10 6
```

WEST	NORTH	EAST	SOUTH
Brother	*George*	*Brother*	*Josie*
Lucius	*Barr*	*Paulo*	*Threlfall*
–	–	–	1◇
1♠	2♡	Pass	3♣
Pass	4♣	Pass	4♠
Pass	5♣	All Pass	

'Your partner's Four Spade bid?' queried Brother Lucius, who was on lead.

'To tell the truth, I was a bit mystified by it,' George Barr replied. 'It may have been to put you off leading a spade.'

Josie Threlfall passed her convention card across the table, tapping a finger on the section marked Slam Bidding. 'We agreed to play Rolling Gerber, George, don't you remember?' she said. 'I was showing you two aces. 4NT by you would be for kings after that, so I took your Five Clubs as a sign-off.'

Brother Lucius led the king of spades and continued with the ace of spades, Paulo playing high-low to indicate an even number of cards in the suit. Since a trump switch might assist declarer, Lucius led a low diamond at trick three. Josie Threlfall won East's queen with the king and placed the ace of trumps on the table.

Brother Paulo was there with his nine, setting up a two-way finesse in the suit, but declarer appeared not to notice the card. She continued with a low trump to dummy's queen, took the marked finesse against East's jack, and drew the last trump. She then cashed two more high diamonds, nodding approvingly at the 3-3 break. 'This must be good, then,' she said, leading her last diamond and throwing a heart from dummy.

'So far, so good,' observed George Barr, smiling encouragingly from across the table.

'Unfortunately, it's not quite enough,' said Mrs Threlfall. She placed the jack of hearts on the table and Lucius covered with the queen, the trick being completed with the ace and nine. When dummy's king of hearts dropped the ten from East, declarer's eight was good.

'You make the last trick,' said Josie Threlfall, facing her ♡8. 'Just the one down. I was expecting a bit more from you, George, after your Gerber bid.'

With some difficulty Brother Paulo managed to keep a straight face. 'Unfortunately for us, your eight of hearts is good,' he said. 'You took an inspired view of the heart suit.'

Mrs Threlfall looked gratefully towards the Italian monk. What a pleasant man he was. Handsome, too. She reached for her scorecard, inserting the 400 with a large tick beside it. 'I had no choice, so far as the hearts were concerned,' she said. 'If I play you for the queen, leading towards the jack, I'd be certain to lose a trick in the suit.'

Back at the other table, the match was nearing its end. The Abbot had just arrived in a somewhat dubious spade game.

North-South game
Dealer West

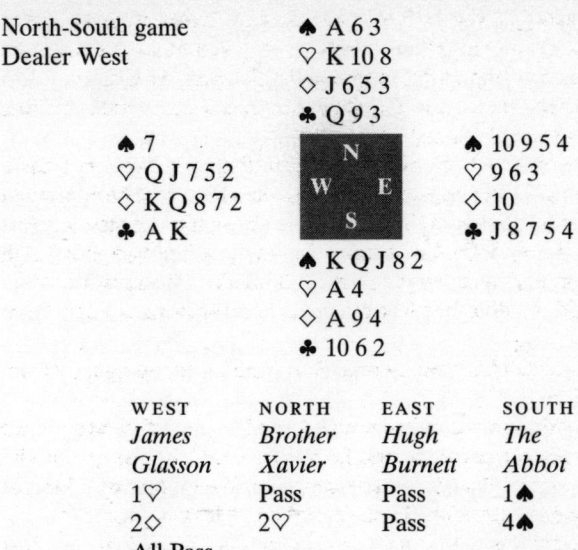

♠ A 6 3
♡ K 10 8
◇ J 6 5 3
♣ Q 9 3

♠ 7
♡ Q J 7 5 2
◇ K Q 8 7 2
♣ A K

♠ 10 9 5 4
♡ 9 6 3
◇ 10
♣ J 8 7 5 4

♠ K Q J 8 2
♡ A 4
◇ A 9 4
♣ 10 6 2

WEST	NORTH	EAST	SOUTH
James	*Brother*	*Hugh*	*The*
Glasson	*Xavier*	*Burnett*	*Abbot*
1♡	Pass	Pass	1♠
2◇	2♡	Pass	4♠
All Pass			

James Glasson cashed two rounds of clubs and switched to the ◇7. The Abbot surveyed the scene uncertainly. What was more likely: that West held the ◇K-Q, or that he held ◇K-10 or ◇Q-10? He had bid twice, it was true. With the jack visible in dummy, though, he would surely have switched to a trump rather than underlead the king-queen of diamonds. 'Play low,' said the Abbot.

The ◇10 appeared from East and the Abbot had to capture immediately to avoid a club ruff. He drew trumps in four rounds and played a club to the queen. A heart to the ace left this position:

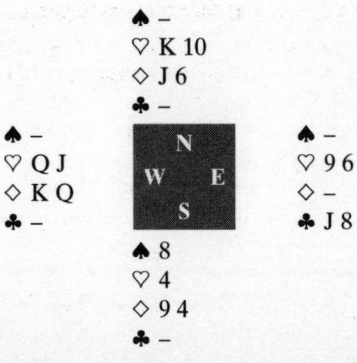

♠ –
♡ K 10
◇ J 6
♣ –

♠ –
♡ Q J
◇ K Q
♣ –

♠ –
♡ 9 6
◇ –
♣ J 8

♠ 8
♡ 4
◇ 9 4
♣ –

When the last trump was led, West spent some time considering his discard. The Abbot, who had resigned himself to defeat, suddenly realised what was happening. West held all the missing honours! Yes, he was squeezed.

West eventually threw the queen of diamonds. 'Throw the heart ten,' instructed the Abbot. A diamond towards the jack set up a tenth trick and the game was made.

The Abbot looked triumphantly across the table, as if he had just beaten some important world record. 'A squeeze without the count!' he announced. If that wasn't a captain's effort, he didn't know what was.

'A fortunate one for you,' observed James Glasson. 'You could have made it easily, just by playing the jack on my diamond switch.'

Hugh Burnett nodded his head in agreement. 'I couldn't believe it when declarer played low,' he remarked. 'You bid diamonds, didn't you?'

The Abbot looked aghast at his two opponents. Did they not realise how rude they were being? If he ever found himself being impolite at the table, he would give up the game immediately. What did winning matches and collecting master points matter, compared with being civil and pleasant to those around you?

'I hope they bid diamonds at the other table,' said James Glasson. 'Josie's bound to put up the jack of diamonds if they do.'

The two teams were soon busy comparing scores. Lucius and Paulo had played a sound second half and the monastery team had recovered the half-time deficit to win the match by 7 IMPs.

'What a shame to lose by such a narrow margin,' said Josie Threlfall, handing the monks their overcoats. 'It's a pity George and I couldn't do as well as we did in the first half. We had four big ticks on our scorecard against the Abbot. Only one in the second half.'

'Are you seeing poor old Bill in hospital tomorrow?' asked Hugh Burnett, his head almost disappearing as he wrapped a second woollen scarf around his neck. 'I'll write down some of the hands if you like and you can take them in for him.

'That's a good idea,' said James Glasson. 'Tell him how the bidding went on the Four Spades hand and I'm sure he'll find the jack of diamonds play.'

7. The Unexpected Visitor

'Brother Herman just phoned to say he will arrive at Winchester station at five o'clock,' said Brother Xavier. 'He'd like you to pick him up.'

The Abbot's mouth fell open. 'Who on earth invited him again?' he said. 'It's the first I've heard about it. Why can't he take a taxi, anyway?'

Since there was no way to contact the Australian monk, the Abbot put in a disgruntled appearance at Winchester station.

'G'day, Abbot,' said Brother Herman, handing his suitcase to the Abbot. 'I've been waiting quite a while.'

The Abbot, who was bent double by the weight of the suitcase, surveyed the Australian disapprovingly. 'Brother Xavier told me five o'clock,' he replied.

'Your trains are normally late, I realise,' Brother Herman replied. 'The London train arrived early on this occasion.'

Not a believer in jet-lag, Brother Herman declared himself available for the monastery pairs that evening. This was an early deal at his table:

Love all
Dealer East

```
                    ♠ K 10 5 2
                    ♡ J 10 6 3
                    ◇ —
                    ♣ 7 6 4 3 2
        ♠ 7                         ♠ Q 9 8 3
        ♡ Q 9 8 4         N         ♡ A 7 5 2
        ◇ A 8 7 4    W         E    ◇ K Q 10 5 2
        ♣ K 9 8 5         S         ♣ —
                    ♠ A J 6 4
                    ♡ K
                    ◇ J 9 6 3
                    ♣ A Q J 10
```

WEST	NORTH	EAST	SOUTH
Brother	*Brother*	*Brother*	*Brother*
Michael	*Gordon*	*Aelred*	*Herman*
–	–	1◇	1NT
Dble	2♣	Pass	2♠
3◇	3♠	Pass	4♠
Pass	Pass	Dble	All Pass

Brother Michael led a low heart against the doubled spade game and down went the dummy.

'I didn't intend my 2♣ bid as Stayman after the double,' said the elderly Brother Gordon. 'I took you for a five-timer in spades when you introduced the suit.'

'What difference does the double make?' demanded Brother Herman. 'Stayman and transfers still apply after a double – that's absolutely standard back in Canberra. Play small.'

Brother Aelred won with the ace of hearts, declarer's king appearing. When a low heart was returned at Trick 2, Brother Herman discarded the queen of clubs. Brother Michael won with the heart queen and played back a club, ruffed by his partner. Brother Aelred scratched his chin as he considered his next play. Three tricks were in the bag. What now? It seemed that the king of diamonds would give nothing away.

Brother Herman ruffed the diamond exit in dummy and discarded the ace and jack of clubs on the two good hearts. He then called for a small club, embarking on a cross-ruff. Realising that he could not afford to let declarer score the low trumps in his hand, Brother Aelred ruffed the club with the eight, forcing declarer's jack. A diamond ruff returned the lead to dummy and these cards remained:

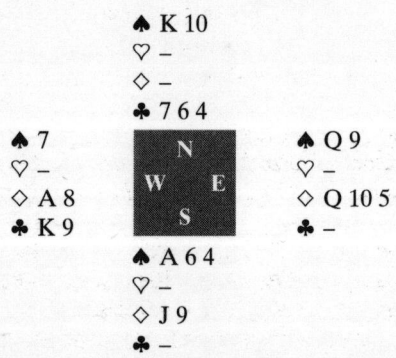

'Play another club,' said Brother Herman.

Brother Aelred sat back in his chair. If he ruffed this club too, declarer would overruff and draw trumps with dummy's king. He would then be able to ruff dummy's last club good and reach it with the ten of trumps. Brother Aelred delayed his fate by discarding a diamond. Brother Herman ruffed with the four, ruffed a diamond with the ten and called for yet another club. Once again East had no good solution. If he threw a diamond, declarer would ruff low and score the last two tricks on a high cross-ruff. When Brother Aelred eventually decided to ruff with the nine, declarer overruffed with the ace. He then played a trump to the king, drawing East's last trump, and claimed the final trick with the established club in dummy.

'Very enjoyable!' declared Brother Herman, reaching for his score-card. 'Ace-queen-jack-ten in clubs and the only club trick I made was with dummy's seven!

'Never mind,' said Brother Gordon. 'You made the contract and that's the main thing.'

The new partnership continued to score well. Halfway through the session they faced the monastery's top pair, Brother Lucius and Brother Paulo.

North-South game
Dealer East

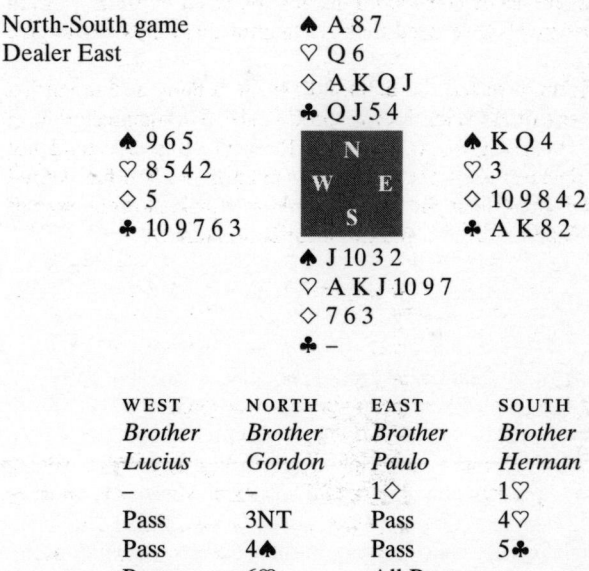

♠ A 8 7
♡ Q 6
♢ A K Q J
♣ Q J 5 4

♠ 9 6 5
♡ 8 5 4 2
♢ 5
♣ 10 9 7 6 3

♠ K Q 4
♡ 3
♢ 10 9 8 4 2
♣ A K 8 2

♠ J 10 3 2
♡ A K J 10 9 7
♢ 7 6 3
♣ –

WEST	NORTH	EAST	SOUTH
Brother	*Brother*	*Brother*	*Brother*
Lucius	*Gordon*	*Paulo*	*Herman*
–	–	1♢	1♡
Pass	3NT	Pass	4♡
Pass	4♠	Pass	5♣
Pass	6♡	All Pass	

Brother Herman had no justification for removing his partner's 3NT bid, particularly when a diamond lead through dummy's holding might result in an adverse ruff. Such considerations did not weigh heavily with him when he had a chance of playing the contract. He decided his heart suit was worth another bid and soon found himself in a small slam.

Brother Lucius led his singleton diamond and down went the dummy. 'Small, please,' said Brother Herman, chuckling to himself as if he were the first player ever to make this minor joke. 'And play a small club.'

If Brother Paulo contributed the ace or king to the trick, declarer would ruff and subsequently take a ruffing finesse in the suit, setting up a second spade discard. It was not a close decision for the Italian. Unless declarer's club cue-bid was based specifically on a singleton ten, it could not gain to go in with an honour. When Brother Paulo played low, the Australian ruffed in the South hand and proceeded to draw trumps in four rounds.

Leaving one trump in his hand, he played off dummy's remaining diamond winners. This end position arose:

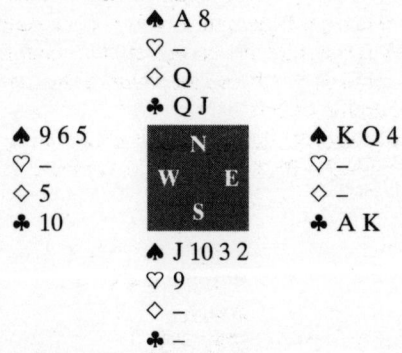

```
              ♠ A 8
              ♡ –
              ◇ Q
              ♣ Q J
  ♠ 9 6 5                    ♠ K Q 4
  ♡ –           N            ♡ –
  ◇ 5       W       E        ◇ –
  ♣ 10          S            ♣ A K
              ♠ J 10 3 2
              ♡ 9
              ◇ –
              ♣ –
```

When the last diamond appeared on the table, Brother Paulo was caught in a trump squeeze without the count. Since it would obviously cost a trick to discard a top club, he threw the four of spades.

'Unless you opened on a 10-count, you should hold both the top spades,' said Brother Herman in a loud voice. 'Play the ace of spades, partner.'

The cards lay as Brother Herman had imagined. Ace and another spade flushed out the two missing spade honours and he claimed the last two tricks with a trump and the established jack of spades.

Brother Gordon reached for the travelling scoresheet. 'It's a complete top for us,' he announced.

'It would only be average-plus back in Canberra,' Brother Herman replied. 'The play could hardly be more obvious. I nearly put in a claim at Trick 1.'

Brother Paulo consulted his watch. 'I hope we don't miss any of the football,' he said. 'The programme starts at 10.40.'

Brother Herman perked up. 'They show Aussie Rules over here, do they?' he asked.

'No, no, it's a Champions League game,' the Italian replied. 'The maestros of Juventus against England's finest, Manchester United.'

'The Raiders are my team,' announced Brother Herman proudly. 'If you ever saw them play, you'd never want to watch soccer again.'

Brother Herman continued to do well and the last round of the evening brought him to the Abbot's table. 'I make us about three tops over, partner,' he said, taking his seat. 'Two more good ones and that should seal it.'

The Abbot reached for his cards with a determined expression. Over my dead body, he thought. How could Brother Herman possibly win the monastery pairs, jet-lagged and with a near senile partner? His estimate of their score must be exaggerated. A couple of bottoms on the last round would probably put them out of the master points. That would shut him up for a while.

Brother Gordon scored a painstakingly slow average in 1NT on the first board. This was the final board of the evening:

```
Game all              ♠ 7 6 4
Dealer North          ♡ 5 2
                      ◇ A K J 8 6 5
                      ♣ A K
   ♠ K Q J 10 2          N          ♠ 9 5
   ♡ K 10 3                         ♡ J 9 7
   ◇ 9 7 3          W       E       ◇ 10 2
   ♣ 4 3               S          ♣ 10 9 7 6 5 2
                      ♠ A 8 3
                      ♡ A Q 8 6 4
                      ◇ Q 4
                      ♣ Q J 8
```

WEST	NORTH	EAST	SOUTH
The	*Brother*	*Brother*	*Brother*
Abbot	*Gordon*	*Xavier*	*Herman*
–	1◇	Pass	1♡
1♠	3◇	Pass	6NT
All Pass			

When his partner indicated a strong hand, Brother Herman headed straight for the top-scoring pairs slam. The Abbot led the king of spades and down went the dummy. 'Ah yes, thank you,' said Brother Herman. 'Very suitable.'

The Abbot's ♠K was allowed to win the first trick and he continued with the ♠Q. Brother Herman won with the ace and cashed dummy's two winners in clubs. A diamond to the queen allowed him to score a third club trick and he returned to dummy with a diamond. When the diamonds were run, this end position arose:

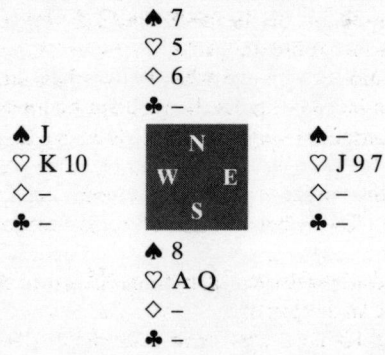

Brother Herman discarded a spade on the last diamond and the Abbot was caught in a simple squeeze. Forced to retain the jack of spades as a guard against dummy's ♠7, he bared the king of hearts.

'I'm not going to get this one wrong, Abbot!' said Brother Herman. He led a heart to the ace and the king fell on his left. The queen of hearts was good for the last trick and the slam had been made.

'Oh dear, oh dear!' Brother Herman exclaimed, shaking his head. 'Not the best of defences, Abbot.'

'Keep your voice down, for Heaven's sake,' said Abbot. 'The other players are trying to concentrate.'

'Lead a diamond and I have no chance,' Brother Herman continued loudly. 'I need the diamond suit for transportation.'

'It's an academic point,' declared the Abbot. 'I had an obvious lead in spades.'

Brother Herman was not listening. 'Suppose I win the diamond lead in hand and cash dummy's two club winners,' he said. 'When I play a spade to the eight and your ten, to rectify the count, you continue with another diamond. There's no squeeze then, do you see? I need to cash the queen of clubs before a squeeze can work.'

'It's another complete top for us,' said Brother Gordon, peering over his glasses at the travelling scoresheet.

'Diamond lead would be automatic back in Canberra,' Brother Herman persisted. 'It's obvious what will happen after a spade lead.'

The Abbot surveyed the Australian in disbelief. It was just about possible to be more obnoxious than he was, but a considerable effort would be required.

An excited Brother Paulo came up to the Abbot's table. 'Half-past ten!' he said. 'In ten minutes we can enjoy the highlights of Juventus against United. You would you like to join us, Brother Herman?'

The Australian shook his head. 'Soccer's a very poor game,' he declared. 'Leaves me completely cold.'

The Abbot could not believe what he was hearing. Had Brother Herman travelled halfway across the globe just to insult the national game of the host country – a game taught to every English boy by his father?

'Look at all the violence you get at your matches,' continued Brother Herman. 'That's because there are so few goals. The crowd gets frustrated.'

Brother Paulo had rarely heard anything so absurd but it was not in his nature to seek an argument.

'The Canberra Raiders won their last game 120-59,' continued Brother Herman, his eyes lighting up at the memory. 'There was no crowd violence at all.'

What a thrilling encounter it must have been, thought the Abbot, the result in doubt until the very last moment.

Brother Herman made his departure and the other monks headed for the lounge, where ITV was rolling the opening credits. The Abbot removed the 'Reserved' sign from a prime chair in the front row and sat down. 'Is Brother Herman completely mad?' he said. 'Can he really believe that football would be more exciting if we had fifty-foot goals, no goalkeeper, and as many scores as in a table tennis match?'

Brother Paulo laughed. 'Don't worry about him, Abbot,' he said. 'Now, who wants a small bet on United? I can't believe they will beat my heroes. Do I have any takers at 2-to-1 against?'

8.   Brother Herman's New Partnership

'This visit has been even worse than the last one,' declared the Abbot. 'When on earth is Brother Herman going back to Australia?'

'Nobody seems to know,' Brother Xavier replied. 'He was with us for a month last time.'

'A month!' exclaimed the Abbot. 'Has he no duties to perform back in Canberra?'

Brother Xavier smiled. 'I expect they're glad to be rid of him,' he suggested. 'The other monks probably get together to save up for his fare.'

'Well, that's another thing,' continued the Abbot. 'How on earth can a religious establishment justify spending so much money on mere recreation? It's not as if he does any work while he's here.'

'We'd better change the subject,' said Brother Xavier. 'Here comes the man himself.'

'Ah, g'day to you both,' said Brother Herman. 'Everyone's happy and healthy back in Canberra, I was pleased to hear.'

'You made a phone call to Australia?' gasped the Abbot. 'Have you any idea how much that costs?'

'No worries, Abbot,' Brother Herman replied. 'Our Monastery of St. Bruce the Divine is on the Internet. I've been keeping in touch by email.'

'You've used my computer!' exclaimed the Abbot. 'It's password-protected. How on earth did you get on to the system?'

Brother Herman laughed. 'Your password didn't delay me for long, Abbot,' he said. 'If you take my advice you'll use a mixture of letters and numbers next time – much harder to crack.'

The Abbot took his seat for the Thursday evening pairs and looked up to see who Brother Herman was playing with. The top half a dozen players in the monastery had been paid a visit by the Abbot and forbidden to partner the Australian. Nevertheless he had managed one first place, with Brother Zac, and one third place – unbelievably – with the ancient Brother Gordon.

A reassuring sight met the Abbot's eyes. Brother Herman was partnering Brother Aelred. Let him get out of that one!

The Abbot started strongly and the fourth round of the event brought Brother Fabius and Brother Zac to his table. Zac was a useful card-player, whereas Fabius had little idea of the game. The Abbot was not in the least surprised when it was Brother Zac who ended as declarer on the first board of the round.

```
Love all               ♠ A 4 3
Dealer South           ♡ Q 6
                       ◇ Q 9 7 3
                       ♣ J 8 5 2
        ♠ K J 10           N          ♠ 9 8 7 2
        ♡ A 8 4                        ♡ 10 3
        ◇ K 8 5 2     W       E        ◇ A J 10 4
        ♣ 10 7 6          S           ♣ 9 4 3
                       ♠ Q 6 5
                       ♡ K J 9 7 5 2
                       ◇ 6
                       ♣ A K Q
```

WEST	NORTH	EAST	SOUTH
The	*Brother*	*Brother*	*Brother*
Abbot	*Fabius*	*Xavier*	*Zac*
–	–	–	1♡
Pass	2♣	Pass	3♡
Pass	4♡	All Pass	

The Abbot led the two of diamonds against Brother Zac's heart game and down went the dummy. 'I nearly responded 1NT,' observed the white-haired Brother Fabius. 'I was worried we might miss game if you held 16 points and passed 1NT.'

If there was one thing the Abbot could not stand, it was dummy waffling on about the bidding. He beckoned to Brother Zac, indicating that he should make his play from the dummy.

'I bid Two Clubs, the lower suit,' continued Brother Fabius, 'even though my clubs were weaker than the diamonds. I believe that's right. It leaves more space for . . .'

'Shall we get on?' intervened the Abbot. 'I'd like to get to bed before midnight, if that's not too inconvenient for you.'

Brother Fabius smiled at the Abbot. 'That shouldn't be a problem,' he replied. 'We normally finish around ten-thirty.'

A low diamond was played from dummy and Brother Xavier won with the ten. When he switched to the nine of spades, Brother Zac played low from the South hand. He was pleased to see the ten appear from the Abbot in the West seat. 'No, no, partner,' he said. 'I don't want the ace. Play low.'

The Abbot, who could not safely continue spades, tried his luck with another low diamond. Declarer ruffed East's jack and played a trump to the queen. If East had held the trump ace, declarer would still have been in trouble. A second round of spades would have removed the entry to dummy and the blocked club winner.

It was not to be. The Abbot held the trump ace and could not attack spades when he won the second round of trumps. He exited with a trump but Brother Zac now claimed the remainder. 'I cash the three clubs, Abbot,' he said, 'and then cross to the ace of spades to play the jack of clubs.'

'Yes, yes, I'm not blind,' grunted the Abbot.

'It was essential to duck the first spade,' Brother Zac explained to his partner. 'If I don't, there's no entry to the jack of clubs.'

'You can't use the queen of trumps as an entry?' queried the ancient Brother Fabius. 'The Abbot had the ace in front of the queen.'

Not for the first time in his life, the Abbot thought what an absurd game bridge could be. Through no fault of his own, the player with the finest brain in the monastery had just conceded a near-top to someone with hardly any brain left at all.

'I think you'll find that doesn't work,' Brother Zac replied.

Brother Fabius leaned forward in a confidential manner. 'I don't like to tell tales, Abbot,' he said, 'but that Australian monk, whatever he's called, he's not very gracious.'

'I don't think you're giving away the world's greatest secret by telling me that,' the Abbot replied.

'I thought I'd played a 3NT contract rather well against him,' Brother Fabius continued. 'All the suits broke badly and I only went one down. He went on for ages, telling me how I should have made it. Gave me quite a headache.'

The Abbot sighed. 'Such poor etiquette doesn't surprise me,' he said. 'We set much higher standards here in England.'

The penultimate round of the evening saw the arrival of Brother Herman at the Abbot's table. The Abbot caught his partner's eye. No foolish mistakes would be tolerated on this particular round. The Australian must be put firmly in his place.

'Ah, it's our distinguished visitor,' said Brother Xavier. 'How's the new partnership faring?'

Brother Herman shook his head. 'Very disappointing,' he replied. 'Very disappointing, indeed.'

The Abbot sucked in his cheeks, enjoying the moment.

'We're two tops over, but it could have been so much better,' the Australian continued. 'Apparently Brother Aelred here doesn't play Reverse Capaletti. It's absolutely standard back in Canberra.'

'I've never heard of it,' declared the Abbot.

'It's a defence to 1NT,' Brother Herman replied. 'It's been scientifically proved to be the best defence. I'll explain it to you later, if we have a moment.'

'Don't trouble yourself,' said the Abbot.

This was the first board of the round:

Love all
Dealer South

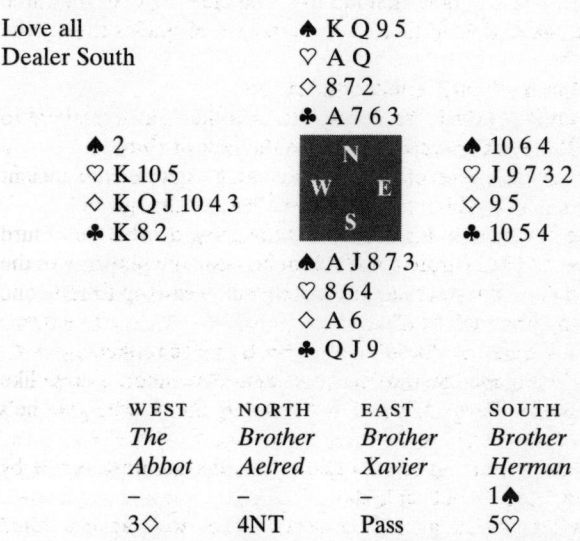

```
              ♠ K Q 9 5
              ♡ A Q
              ◇ 8 7 2
              ♣ A 7 6 3
♠ 2                          ♠ 10 6 4
♡ K 10 5            N        ♡ J 9 7 3 2
◇ K Q J 10 4 3   W   E       ◇ 9 5
♣ K 8 2            S         ♣ 10 5 4
              ♠ A J 8 7 3
              ♡ 8 6 4
              ◇ A 6
              ♣ Q J 9
```

WEST	NORTH	EAST	SOUTH
The	*Brother*	*Brother*	*Brother*
Abbot	*Aelred*	*Xavier*	*Herman*
–	–	–	1♠
3◇	4NT	Pass	5♡
Pass	6♠	All Pass	

The Abbot led the king of diamonds and Brother Aelred laid out his dummy. 'I don't know if you agree with my Blackwood bid,' he said. 'I thought I was worth one try with a fifteen-count.'

The Abbot looked despairingly to the ceiling. What an appalling 4NT bid, particularly as he had no diamond control. It was absolutely typical that Brother Herman should rescue the situation by turning up with the diamond ace.

The Australian ducked the first round of diamonds and won the second. A finesse of the heart queen succeeded and he cashed the ace of hearts. After drawing two rounds of trumps with the king and ace, he ruffed a heart with the queen. Two more rounds of trumps left these cards outstanding:

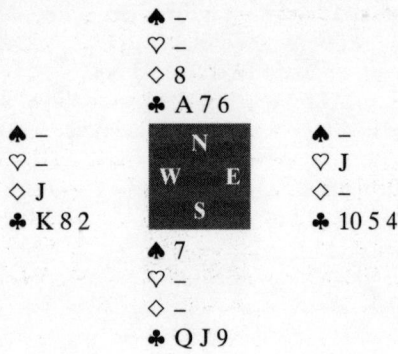

```
                    ♠ –
                    ♡ –
                    ◇ 8
                    ♣ A 7 6
    ♠ –                         ♠ –
    ♡ –          N              ♡ J
    ◇ J       W     E           ◇ –
    ♣ K 8 2      S              ♣ 10 5 4
                    ♠ 7
                    ♡ –
                    ◇ –
                    ♣ Q J 9
```

When declarer's last trump appeared on the table, the Abbot had to throw a club to retain his diamond guard. 'Diamond away,' said Brother Herman.

The queen of clubs was covered by the king and ace. Brother Herman had a count on the club suit and now had to guess which defender had started with the club ten. If the card lay with East, a finesse of the nine would land the slam. If the Abbot had started with K-10-x in the suit, the ten would now drop. The clubs had started 3-3 but since the Abbot had shown up with the king, Brother Herman assessed the odds as 3-to-2 in favour of East holding the ten. 'Small club,' he said.

A finesse of the nine succeeded and the slam had been made.

'Well done, partner,' said Brother Aelred. 'I thought I'd have enough for you.'

Brother Xavier had not followed the hand very closely. 'Was that right to cover the club queen, Abbot?' he said. 'You set up a finesse against my ten.'

'I only had two clubs left, for Heaven's sake,' the Abbot reprimanded. 'He knows that. If I don't cover, he plays low to the ace on the next round and makes it even if you started with 10-9-x in the suit.'

'Yes, yes, of course,' apologised Brother Xavier. 'I was half asleep.'

Brother Aelred inspected the scoresheet proudly. 'We're the only ones in a slam,' he reported. 'The other Norths must have been too timid in the bidding.'

'It's only the Abbot's overcall that makes the slam good,' Brother
Herman replied. 'That's why I don't like to intervene on a minor suit.
The 50-50 finesses became near certainties.'

The Abbot was hoping for revenge as he drew his cards for the
second board of the round.

Game all
Dealer East

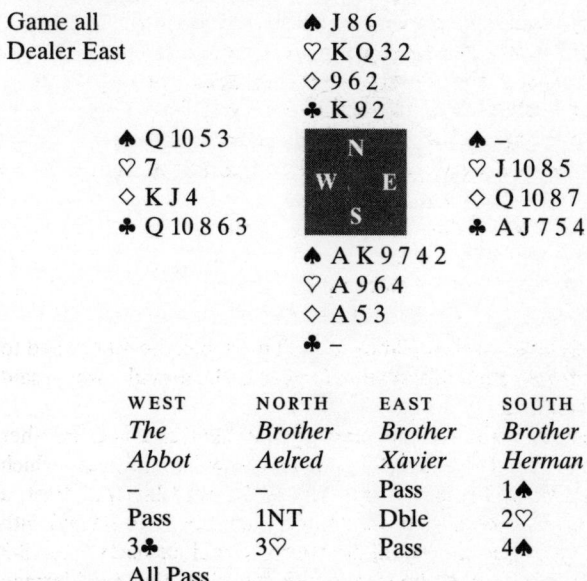

```
              ♠ J 8 6
              ♡ K Q 3 2
              ◇ 9 6 2
              ♣ K 9 2
♠ Q 10 5 3              ♠ –
♡ 7                    ♡ J 10 8 5
◇ K J 4                ◇ Q 10 8 7
♣ Q 10 8 6 3           ♣ A J 7 5 4
              ♠ A K 9 7 4 2
              ♡ A 9 6 4
              ◇ A 5 3
              ♣ –
```

WEST	NORTH	EAST	SOUTH
The Abbot	*Brother Aelred*	*Brother Xavier*	*Brother Herman*
–	–	Pass	1♠
Pass	1NT	Dble	2♡
3♣	3♡	Pass	4♠
All Pass			

With a trump holding that might fare well in its own right, the Abbot
embarked on a forcing game rather than leading his singleton. Brother
Herman covered the ♣6 lead with dummy's nine and Brother Xavier
played the jack. After a few seconds thought the Australian monk
discarded a diamond from his hand.

Brother Herman won the diamond switch with the ace and cashed
the ace of trumps, East throwing a club. When a second round of
trumps was led towards the dummy, the Abbot rose with the queen. It
was tempting in a way to cash the king of diamonds at this stage but
the Abbot did not favour this line of defence. It was fairly obvious
from declarer's 2♡ rebid that it would set up a heart-club squeeze
against East. Refusing to rectify the count for declarer, the Abbot
returned the queen of clubs. 'Play low,' said Brother Herman, ruffing
in his hand.

After a trump to the bare jack Brother Herman needed to reach his hand to draw the outstanding trump. He could not afford to ruff the ♣K, a valuable threat card, so he would have to play a heart. West was more or less marked with a singleton in the suit, after East's take-out double. Brother Herman's eventual intention was to end-play East with a club, forcing him to lead away from a heart honour. If West had started with a singleton heart honour, a heart to the ace would be right at this stage. If West instead held a low singleton, declarer would have to steel himself for a finesse of the nine. This was the percentage play, in fact. 'Small heart, please,' said Brother Herman.

Brother Xavier hesitated for a moment and then inserted the jack of hearts. This was very much to Brother Herman's liking. He won with the ace and drew the last trump, East throwing a diamond. These cards remained:

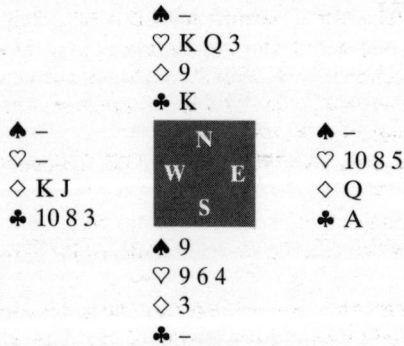

```
              ♠ —
              ♡ K Q 3
              ◇ 9
              ♣ K
  ♠ —                      ♠ —
  ♡ —          N           ♡ 10 8 5
  ◇ K J     W     E        ◇ Q
  ♣ 10 8 3     S           ♣ A
              ♠ 9
              ♡ 9 6 4
              ◇ 3
              ♣ —
```

Brother Herman led his last trump, throwing a diamond from dummy. 'It doesn't matter what you play,' he said, turning towards Brother Xavier.

When Brother Xavier released the ◇Q, the Australian crossed to the table with a heart and threw him in with a club. At Trick 12 a heart lead away from the ten gave declarer his game.

'It didn't cost, splitting the hearts,' said Brother Herman. 'I'd made up my mind to finesse the nine anyway.' He turned towards the Abbot. 'It was your opening lead that cost it.'

The Abbot had rarely encountered such poor etiquette at the table. It might be normal practice at St Bruce the whatever but it was quite unacceptable here in England. 'If you mean I should lead a heart, that's an absurd suggestion,' he retorted. 'With four good trumps any expert would lead a club.'

'Of course,' Brother Herman replied. 'You should lead the queen or ten, though. If I duck then, you can play a second club through the king.'

'It's all irrelevant,' the Abbot declared. 'Five Clubs is frigid, Xavier. Why on earth didn't you raise me with five-card support and a void spade?'

'You can't make Five Clubs on a spade lead,' said Brother Herman. 'You have to ruff and we can force the dummy again in spades when we take the red aces. You can't pick up the trump king then.'

'Obviously,' declared the Abbot. 'Brother Aelred would have led the king of hearts, though, and eleven tricks are easy then.'

The session drew to a close and after a quick pint in the Buttery the Abbot headed for his study in order to change his computer password. When he first bought the machine he had deliberately chosen a very long password, one with a full eleven letters in it. How in Heaven's name could anyone manage to guess such a password? Brother Herman wouldn't even *know* that he was a grandmaster. It wasn't as if he went around bragging about it.

The Abbot entered his study and could not believe the sight before him.

'Only me,' said Brother Herman. 'I won't be long.'

'Do you realise what the time is?' thundered the Abbot. 'It's nearly midnight.'

'Yes, yes, I just have a few things to check on the Internet,' the Australian replied. 'I won't be more than fifteen minutes.'

The Abbot retired to his cell but was unable to sleep. It was absolutely intolerable that Brother Herman should monopolise the computer, the sole purpose of which was to advance charitable works. Apart from that, he had wanted to set off some pirate music downloads before retiring for the night. He was still missing two parts of Bach's Mass in B minor and he needed to burn the CD by tomorrow to send as a friend's birthday present. He would have to set his alarm clock for half an hour before Mattins and request the downloads then. If Brother Herman was still on the machine at that time he would throttle him, that's what he'd do. For a person like that . . . no other punishment was good enough!

9.   Brother Herman's Announcement

The Abbot was taking a morning stroll around the quadrangle when he spotted the Australian monk, Brother Herman, approaching him. No means of escape offered itself and he quickened his pace, hoping to give the impression that he was on his way somewhere important.

'G'day, Abbot!' said Brother Herman. 'I see you've taken my advice about changing your computer password. Unfortunately it meant that I couldn't use your machine this morning.' He handed the Abbot an old bridge scorecard. 'Perhaps you could jot down the new password for me.'

The Abbot brushed the scorecard aside. 'That machine is for official monastery use only,' he replied. 'It's the only way that we can justify it being tax deductible.'

Brother Herman laughed. 'Yes, yes, we work the same fiddle at St Bruce's,' he said. 'I notice that it doesn't prevent you from downloading music from the WINMX site.'

'That music is er . . . to comfort those monks suffering in the infirmary,' the Abbot replied. 'You know full well that I have no spare time for listening to music. Anyway, I'm afraid I'm in a hurry. I'll speak to you later.'

The Abbot managed to avoid any further encounter until the evening's duplicate pairs. He looked around the room to see if Brother Herman had managed to persuade anyone to partner him. On the previous session, most annoyingly, he had managed to drag Brother Aelred into second place. It was unbelievable. The highest place Brother Aelred had achieved previously, in thirty years play, was fourth. That had been during the great flu epidemic of 1986 when only five pairs had played.

The Abbot strained his eyes to look at the occupants of Table 9 in the far corner. Good grief! The obnoxious novice, Brother Cameron, was sitting opposite the Australian. A partnership made in hell if ever there was one.

Round 7 brought the new pairing to the Abbot's table. 'It's very good of you to give one of our youngsters a game,' he declared, as Brother Herman took his seat.

'Not at all,' the Australian replied. 'Brother Cameron is a very strong player. We've wiped the floor with most of the opponents so far.'

The Abbot summoned his concentration. If any floor-wiping was to occur on this round he would perform it himself.

Game all
Dealer East

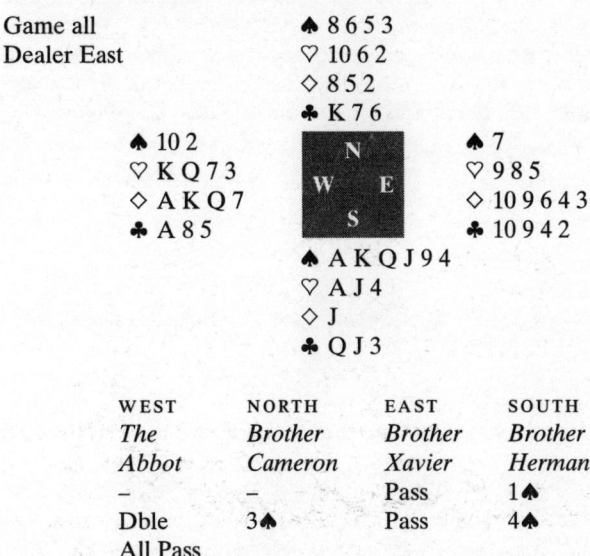

	♠ 8 6 5 3	
	♡ 10 6 2	
	◇ 8 5 2	
	♣ K 7 6	
♠ 10 2		♠ 7
♡ K Q 7 3		♡ 9 8 5
◇ A K Q 7		◇ 10 9 6 4 3
♣ A 8 5		♣ 10 9 4 2
	♠ A K Q J 9 4	
	♡ A J 4	
	◇ J	
	♣ Q J 3	

WEST	NORTH	EAST	SOUTH
The	*Brother*	*Brother*	*Brother*
Abbot	*Cameron*	*Xavier*	*Herman*
–	–	Pass	1♠
Dble	3♠	Pass	4♠
All Pass			

The Abbot led the king of diamonds against the spade game and stared in disbelief at the dummy laid down by Brother Cameron. 'That's a twelve-loser hand,' he gasped. 'How can you justify a double raise?'

'We play it as pre-emptive,' the novice replied.

'The whole world plays it as pre-emptive!' retorted the Abbot. 'That doesn't mean you should invite 800 on a twelve-loser hand.'

'A very old-fashioned attitude, if I may say so, Abbot,' declared Brother Herman. 'With a likely total of nine trumps you should bid to the nine-trick level immediately.'

The Abbot beckoned for play to continue. 'You're both as mad as each other,' he said.

Brother Xavier signalled with the three of diamonds on the first trick, indicating an odd number of diamonds. When the jack fell from declarer, the Abbot was inclined to believe that the card was a singleton. To continue with a second round of diamonds would assist declarer in preparing for an elimination. Since entries to dummy were scarce it must be a stronger defence to switch elsewhere.

At Trick 2 the Abbot switched to a trump. Brother Herman won with the nine and drew the outstanding trump with the ace. When he continued with the queen of clubs the Abbot won with the ace. Still refusing to assist declarer by playing another diamond, he exited with a club.

Brother Herman won in the dummy and ruffed a diamond with the king, retaining his four of trumps. He cashed one more high trump, followed by the jack of clubs, leaving these cards still to be played:

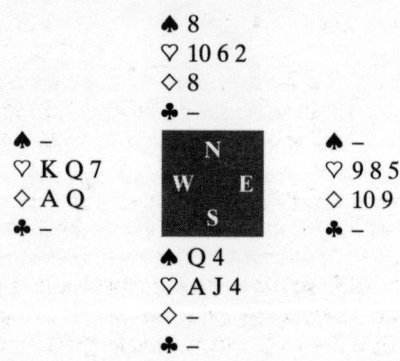

When Brother Herman led the four of trumps the Abbot had no good card to play in the West seat. If he threw a heart it would be easy for declarer to set up two tricks in the suit. Eventually he parted with the ace of diamonds and the trick was won with dummy's eight of trumps. 'Play the diamond,' said Brother Herman.

The Australian ruffed with his last trump, leaving the Abbot with K-Q-7 of hearts. A low heart from the South hand forced him to win and lead away from his remaining honour. The game had been made.

'Nice one, partner!' congratulated Brother Cameron. 'Some sort of squeeze without the count, was it?'

'A very common variation,' Brother Herman replied. 'I see it almost every week back in Canberra.'

The Abbot was hoping for better things as he drew his cards for the next board:

Love all   ♠ K 7
Dealer South   ♡ Q 5 4
                  ◇ K Q 8 7 5
                  ♣ K 6 3

♠ 6	**N**	♠ 9 5 4 2
♡ K J 10 9 7 2	**W E**	♡ 6 3
◇ A J 10 6	**S**	◇ 9 3 2
♣ Q 5		♣ J 10 8 7

                  ♠ A Q J 10 8 3
                  ♡ A 8
                  ◇ 4
                  ♣ A 9 4 2

WEST	NORTH	EAST	SOUTH
The	*Brother*	*Brother*	*Brother*
Abbot	*Cameron*	*Xavier*	*Herman*
–	–	–	1♠
2♡	3NT	Pass	6♠
All Pass			

'Your partner's 3NT bid?' queried the Abbot, who was on lead.

'A sound balanced raise to game in spades,' Brother Herman replied. 'Assuming we're on the same wavelength.'

The Abbot spent some time considering his opening lead. A club lead was out of the question. As for the leads in the other three suits, they seemed equally dangerous. Muttering a small prayer, he reached for his singleton trump.

Brother Cameron looked somewhat apprehensive as he laid out his dummy. 'My response was a two-way bid,' he explained. 'It could be taken as natural but since partner is likely to hold five spades it could also be taken as a sound balanced raise to game in spades.'

'Stop waffling!' exclaimed the Abbot. 'It's entirely obvious that you meant it as natural and I was given the wrong explanation.'

'We haven't played together before, Abbot,' said Brother Cameron. 'I thought I should . . .'

'Let's get on with the play, for Heaven's sake,' continued the Abbot. 'The score can be adjusted at the end, if need be.'

Brother Herman won the trump lead in the South hand and advanced his singleton diamond. Twelve tricks would have been easy if the Abbot had risen with the ace, since declarer could have scored three diamond tricks. He defended strongly by playing low and dummy's king of diamonds won the trick. Brother Herman ruffed a diamond, returned to dummy with the king of trumps and ruffed another diamond. Disappointed that the ace of diamonds had not yet appeared, he drew East's remaining trumps. This position had been reached:

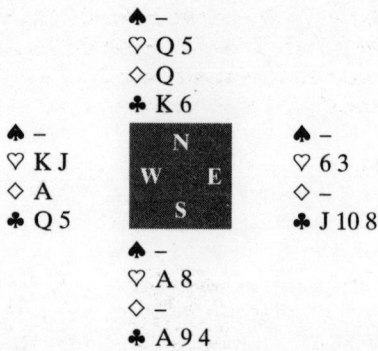

Brother Herman was in no doubt how to continue. He cashed the ace and king of clubs, removing the Abbot's holding in that suit, and then exited with the queen of diamonds. The Abbot won with the ace and had to lead away from the king of hearts. Brother Herman scored the queen and ace of hearts and the small slam had been made.

The Abbot slumped back in his chair. 'Appallingly lucky!' he exclaimed. 'You bid the slam on a complete misunderstanding and then you find all the cards lying right.'

'A club lead beats it, I think,' observed Brother Xavier.

Perking up at this news, the Abbot turned towards Brother Herman. 'That's right,' he said. 'You win the club lead with the ace and play a diamond. I rise with the ace and play a second club, removing the late entry to dummy. You can throw two losers on the diamond king-queen but you still have one loser left.'

Brother Herman waved a finger in his partner's direction, indicating that he should fill in the travelling scoresheet.

'Wait a minute,' declared the Abbot. 'There's no way I would have led a singleton trump unless I'd been told that the dummy held strong spade support. There would be too much chance of trapping an honour in partner's hand. A red-suit lead is out of the question, so I'd be forced to try a club. Since I was seriously misinformed on the bidding, we'll have to score it as one down.'

Seeking guidance, Brother Cameron looked at his partner.

'What on earth are you looking at him for?' demanded the Abbot. 'Just because he's not English, you can't get away with a faulty explanation of the bidding. The Laws of Bridge apply equally in both hemispheres.'

Brother Cameron reluctantly inscribed the result as one down and the next board was brought into position.

'Strictly speaking, you should also be fined 20% of a top,' continued the Abbot, as he sorted his cards for the next board. 'As it's just a friendly local duplicate, we'll let that pass.'

This was the final board of the round:

```
North-South game          ♠ 10 9
Dealer North              ♡ A 7 2
                          ◇ A K 10 6 5
                          ♣ A 6 2
        ♠ 8 6 5 3          N          ♠ 4
        ♡ J 6 5       W         E      ♡ K Q 10 8 3
        ◇ 8 3                          ◇ Q J 9 7 2
        ♣ Q J 10 3         S          ♣ 8 5
                          ♠ A K Q J 7 2
                          ♡ 9 4
                          ◇ 4
                          ♣ K 9 7 4
```

WEST	NORTH	EAST	SOUTH
The	*Brother*	*Brother*	*Brother*
Abbot	*Cameron*	*Xavier*	*Herman*
–	1◇	1♡	1♠
Pass	1NT	Pass	3♠
Pass	4♣	Pass	4◇
Pass	4♡	Dble	Pass
Pass	Rdble	Pass	4NT
Pass	5♣	Pass	6♠
All Pass			

The Abbot led the three of trumps and down went the dummy. Brother Herman gave a small shake of the head as he assessed his prospects. On any other lead he could have played ace, king and another club, ruffing the fourth round of the suit. How on earth had the Abbot found the trump lead? Still, if the diamonds were 4-3 he would be able to set up a twelfth trick there.

Brother Herman won the first trick with dummy's ten of trumps. He then cashed the ace and king of diamonds, discarding a heart. When he ruffed a diamond with the ace, he was disappointed to see West show out. What could be done now?

The odds were good that East's shape was 1-5-5-2 or 1-6-5-1. In that case the contract could be made if a club could be ducked into the East hand. Brother Xavier would have no trump to play and a club ruff would still be possible!

At Trick 5 Brother Herman led a low club from his hand, the Abbot following with the three. 'Play the six,' he said.

Brother Xavier won with the eight in the East seat but had no trump remaining, as declarer had foreseen. When he switched to the king of hearts, Brother Herman won with dummy's ace and continued with the ace and king of clubs. A fourth round of clubs was ruffed with dummy's nine. The Australian then crossed to his hand with a heart ruff and drew trumps. 'They're all there now,' he said.

'Not the best, Abbot,' observed Brother Xavier. 'Can't you put in a higher club to stop him ducking the trick to me?'

The Abbot glared across the table. How could anyone imagine that declarer would put in the six? He might have worked out the right defence in a Gold Cup match, where you could think for ages on every hand. In a local duplicate it was rank bad manners to delay the play in that way.

'Makes no difference at all,' said Brother Herman. 'If the Abbot puts in a high club I win with dummy's ace, ruff a heart, cross to dummy's remaining trump and ruff another heart. I can then end-play the Abbot with the nine of clubs, pinning your eight.'

The Abbot sucked in his cheeks at this reprieve. 'That's the play I feared,' he declared. 'The only hope was to play low on the club and hope that Brother Herman went wrong. Did you follow that, Xavier?'

'Move for the next round,' called the voice of Brother Zac from across the room.

As Brother Herman rose to his feet the Abbot grasped the sleeve of his cassock. 'Pleasant as it is to have you here,' he said, 'I don't believe you've told us the date of your return flight.'

'I'm afraid I'm going to have to disappoint you all, Abbot,' Brother Herman replied. 'I realise that everyone's enjoyed my visit and I've had a great time myself but, well, my plane leaves Heathrow at 9.45 tomorrow morning.'

The Abbot could not disguise the look of ecstasy that came to his face. It had been a gruelling three weeks but at last life could return to normal.

'The trains are very inconvenient, so I'll need a lift to the airport,' Brother Herman continued. 'The check-in is at 6.45, Abbot, and your car is not of the speediest. We'll have to leave around five o'clock, I reckon!'

10.   The Inappropriate Opponents

'I have the draw for the second round of the Cahalan Cup,' said the Abbot, studying a sheet of paper in his hand. 'We're playing at home against er . . . F. Hargreaves. Never heard of him.'

'Neither have I,' Brother Xavier replied. 'What's the address?'

The Abbot surveyed the list of captains' addresses. 'Ah, that explains it,' he said. 'Southampton University. We've played against that sort of team many a time. The odd flash of brilliance but no idea of the game in general. I'll be disappointed if they don't concede after three sets.'

Two weeks later, on the appointed day, a blue MG pulled up outside the monastery gates. The Abbot, who was surveying proceedings from an upper window, could not believe the sight before him. Not only were the opponents all young girls, they were distastefully clad in the extreme. Had they no idea that they would be playing in a monastery? Apart from the impropriety of the situation, there was no way Brother Xavier would be able to retain his concentration. It was well known that anything remotely female distracted him.

The visitors were soon being welcomed through the portals. 'Are you the Abbot, then?' said Fabia Hargreaves, whose jeans had been scissored some twelve inches above the knee.

'I am,' replied the Abbot. 'And this is the ancient monastery of St Titus . . . not some Caribbean beach.'

'Yes, we found it OK,' said Debbie Locke-Taylor. She took a few steps forward, gazing admiringly at the cloisters. 'Hey, look at that! Neat, isn't it?'

The four girls were quickly ushered into the senior card room before any St Titus novice could catch a glimpse of them. The match began and this was an early board at the Abbot's table.

Love all
Dealer West

```
              ♠ A J 9 8
              ♡ 4 3
              ◇ A 10 9 2
              ♣ A 5 2
♠ 4 2                           ♠ 6 5
♡ K J 10 9 7 6 2               ♡ 8 5
◇ J 8                          ◇ Q 7 6 3
♣ 10 9                         ♣ Q J 8 6 3
              ♠ K Q 10 7 3
              ♡ A Q
              ◇ K 5 4
              ♣ K 7 4
```

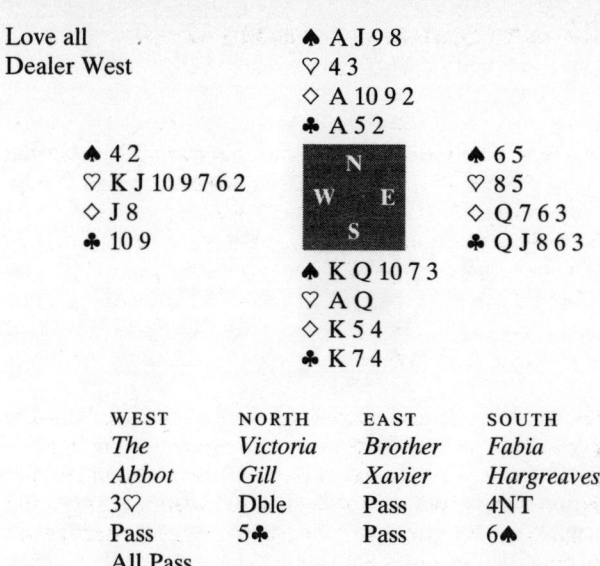

WEST	NORTH	EAST	SOUTH
The	*Victoria*	*Brother*	*Fabia*
Abbot	*Gill*	*Xavier*	*Hargreaves*
3♡	Dble	Pass	4NT
Pass	5♣	Pass	6♠
All Pass			

The Abbot gazed surreptitiously at the slender South player. What amazing lilac eyes she had. Xavier was sure to spend more time gawking at these opponents than looking at his cards. His attention span was limited at the best of times. There was an enticing perfume in the air, too. Jasmine, was it? It took him back some forty years, to that red-haired girl he had dated at the Guildford Tennis Club, just before going to theological college. What was her name? Jane something.

'It's your lead, Abbot,' said Brother Xavier.

'Is it?' exclaimed the Abbot.

The Abbot led the ♣10 against the spade slam and the young declarer won in her hand. After drawing trumps in two rounds, she surveyed the dummy with an air of disappointment. What chance was there of twelve tricks? If West had 2-7-3-1 shape with ◇Q-J-x, she could end-play him on the third round of diamonds. He would have to lead a heart into the tenace and the club loser would go on the thirteenth diamond.

Fabia Hargreaves led a second round of clubs to test the situation there. When the Abbot followed to a second club, declarer had to abandon her first plan. If West held seven hearts for his pre-empt, it was no longer possible for him to hold three diamonds. She played the two top diamonds, interested to see an honour falling from the Abbot's hand. This position had been reached:

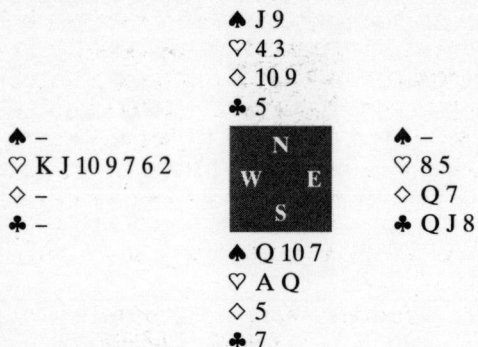

```
                    ♠ J 9
                    ♡ 4 3
                    ◇ 10 9
                    ♣ 5
    ♠ -                              ♠ -
    ♡ K J 10 9 7 6 2                 ♡ 8 5
    ◇ -                              ◇ Q 7
    ♣ -                              ♣ Q J 8
                    ♠ Q 10 7
                    ♡ A Q
                    ◇ 5
                    ♣ 7
```

Declarer now played the ace and queen of hearts, throwing the Abbot on lead. When the enforced heart return came, she ruffed in the dummy and discarded the last diamond in her hand. A ruffing finesse in diamonds set up a winner in the suit and away went declarer's losing club. The slam had been made.

The Abbot blinked. His earlier words about the 'odd flash of brilliance' had certainly been prophetic. Still, if truth be told there was no other way to play the slam. Surely a pair of inveterate overbidders such as Lucius and Paulo would find their way to the six-level. It should be a flat board.

'What happens if he lets the queen of hearts win?' asked Victoria Gill, who was wearing an alarmingly thin yellow tee-shirt.

'I go one down,' her partner replied. 'Still, it's not an easy defence to find.'

'I did give you my count in the minors,' said Brother Xavier.

The Abbot paused to recall the ending. Good grief, they were right! If he had simply allowed declarer to win the second round of hearts, she would have been left with two minor-suit losers. Had he been distracted by the unaccustomed presence of young females? Hard as this was to believe, it was the only possible reason for his defence. When had he ever made such a mistake before?

Meanwhile, at the other table, Lucius and Paulo had been finding the going difficult against their opponents. The players withdrew their cards for this board:

North-South game
Dealer South

```
                    ♠ 10 5 4
                    ♡ K 7 4
                    ◇ A K J 8
                    ♣ K 7 3
    ♠ A 7                          ♠ Q J 9 3
    ♡ Q J 10 5 3      N            ♡ 9 8 2
    ◇ 7 6 4        W     E         ◇ 10 5 3 2
    ♣ 10 6 5          S            ♣ 8 4
                    ♠ K 8 6 2
                    ♡ A 6
                    ◇ Q 9
                    ♣ A Q J 9 2
```

WEST	NORTH	EAST	SOUTH
Brother	*Emma*	*Brother*	*Debbie*
Lucius	*Smith*	*Paulo*	*Locke-Taylor*
–	–	–	1♣
1♡	Dble	Pass	2♠
Pass	3♡	Pass	3NT
Pass	6NT	All Pass	

Brother Lucius led the ♡Q against the no-trump slam, Brother Paulo contributing the two to show three cards in the suit. Debbie Locke-Taylor, an unusually tall girl, eyed the dummy with an academic expression. Only eleven tricks on top and West's overcall on a queen-high suit rather suggested that he would hold the ace of spades. What could she do about it?

All would be easy if West had started with six hearts, giving him the sole heart guard. Nine winners in the minors would force him to reduce to two hearts and the bare spade ace. A low spade would then set up declarer's ♠K. East's ♡2 signal had not passed unnoticed by the young declarer, however. With the hearts apparently breaking 5-3, it was not so easy to see how twelve tricks might be made. Ah well, there was no real alternative to running the minor suits first.

Declarer won the heart lead in her hand and proceeded to run dummy's diamonds, followed by her clubs. This end position arose:

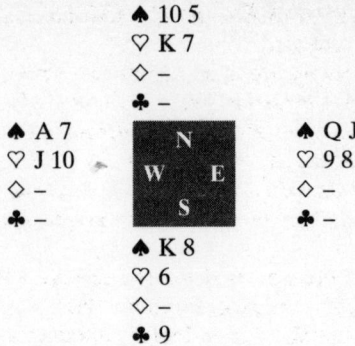

```
              ♠ 10 5
              ♡ K 7
              ♦ –
              ♣ –
♠ A 7                      ♠ Q J
♡ J 10        N            ♡ 9 8
♦ –       W       E        ♦ –
♣ –           S            ♣ –
              ♠ K 8
              ♡ 6
              ♦ –
              ♣ 9
```

When Debbie Locke-Taylor played her last club winner, Brother Lucius could see his fate if he threw a spade. Hoping for the best, he discarded ♡10 instead. A spade was thrown from dummy and Brother Paulo realised that he had no choice to make. Since Lucius had abandoned the heart suit, he would have to retain a heart guard himself, throwing the jack of spades.

The young declarer paused to check her calculations. East had thrown the nine and jack of spades and now held only one more spade. It could hardly be the ace or West would have overcalled on a five-count. In any case it would not help her to find East with a bare ace at this stage. No, she would have to play him for the bare queen.

A heart to dummy's king removed West's last card in that suit and the ♠10 was led from dummy. It was covered in quick turn by the queen, king and ace. At Trick 13 Brother Lucius had to return the ♠7 to declarer's ♠8. The slam had been made

'You made the eight of spades, Debbie?' exclaimed the North player. 'That was clever.'

Lucius and Paulo looked at each other. Without realising what she was doing, the young girl had executed a vice squeeze. Brother Lucius could hardly believe it. Despite having read all the books on squeeze-play ever written, he had not once spotted the chance to make a play like that. It was rather a shame that the opportunity had fallen to someone who had no idea what she was doing.

Debbie Locke-Taylor smiled at her partner. 'Prospects didn't look very good after West's overcall,' she said. 'With the ace of spades marked offside, the vice squeeze was the only chance.'

The Abbot was not in the least amused to find the Monastery team 18 IMPs adrift after the first set. 'Just because the opponents have no idea about the game,' he informed his team mates, 'it doesn't mean that we can afford to relax.'

'They're not so bad as you think,' Brother Lucius replied. 'That tall girl played very strongly against us.'

The Abbot peered over his glasses at Brother Lucius. 'Such terms are relative,' he declared. 'A 19-year-old girl playing strongly is equivalent to one of us playing on a bad day. If we don't pick up 40 IMPs or so on the next set, we can wave goodbye to any thoughts of an early concession.'

The opponents were switched for the second set and the Abbot found himself eyeing the player whose dummy play Lucius had admired. She was a striking good-looker, it had to be admitted, with the most amazing chestnut-coloured hair. No doubt Lucius had let this override his judgement about how good her card-play was.

After a few mundane exchanges, this board arrived:

```
Game all              ♠ A K Q 7 5 3
Dealer South          ♡ 7 4
                      ◇ K J
                      ♣ K Q J
   ♠ 4                              ♠ J 9 8 2
   ♡ A Q J 10 8 6 5      N          ♡ 9 2
   ◇ 8               W     E        ◇ 10 9 7 6 4 3
   ♣ 10 9 8 4           S           ♣ 6
                      ♠ 10 6
                      ♡ K 3
                      ◇ A Q 5 2
                      ♣ A 7 5 3 2
```

WEST	NORTH	EAST	SOUTH
Brother	*Emma*	*The*	*Debbie*
Xavier	*Smith*	*Abbot*	*Locke-Taylor*
–	–	–	1♣
3♡	3♠	Pass	3NT
Pass	4NT	Pass	5♡
Pass	6NT	All Pass	

Seeking a safe lead, Brother Xavier led the ♣10 against 6NT. Debbie Locke-Taylor surveyed the riches laid out in the dummy. Twelve tricks were probably available but the annoying blockages in the minors might prevent her from enjoying them all. If the spades broke 3-2, all would be well. A 3-2 club break would be good enough, too. She could then cash dummy's two diamond honours and overtake the third round of clubs.

The young South player won the club lead in the dummy and called for another top club. East showed out on the second round, throwing a diamond, and one of declarer's life-lines had been lost. After cashing dummy's remaining club honour, Debbie Locke-Taylor played the king of diamonds and overtook the jack of diamonds with the queen, West showing out. A fourth round of clubs left these cards still to be played:

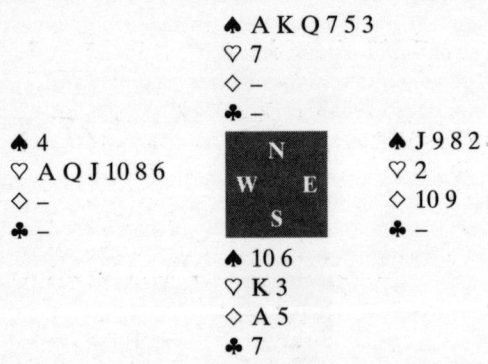

Declarer led her last club, throwing the ♡7 from dummy. The Abbot, sitting East, could not afford to discard a spade or a diamond. Like it or not, he had to throw the ♡2, killing the link to his partner's hand.

Debbie Locke-Taylor paused to review the situation. East was known to hold two diamonds at this stage. West surely held seven hearts for his vulnerable overcall, so that left East with four spades. Unless West's singleton spade was the jack, she would be able to duck a spade into the safe East hand.

When declarer led the ♠10 from her hand, Brother Xavier followed impotently with the ♠4. 'Play low,' said Debbie Locke-Taylor.

The Abbot won with the ten and could see that a spade return would give the remaining tricks to the dummy. He exited with a diamond instead but, as he had feared, this provided no relief. Declarer won with the ace and led her remaining spade to the winners in dummy. The notrump slam had been made.

The Abbot felt as if he were in the middle of some weird dream. Could this girl really be a student? She looked more like some beautiful alien from outer space, programmed to play the winning card at every turn. That was the only possible explanation. It went beyond all logic that a young girl, with more legs than sense, should play bridge at such a level.

'Spade lead beats it, I think,' said Debbie Locke-Taylor.

The Abbot perked up. How many times had Xavier made similar observations at his expense? It was no more than justice that he should receive a taste of his own medicine. 'I didn't like to point it out to him myself,' he informed the declarer. 'As soon as dummy went down, I was wishing that we'd had a spade lead.'

A few boards later, the 19-year-old was in a vulnerable game.

Game all
Dealer South

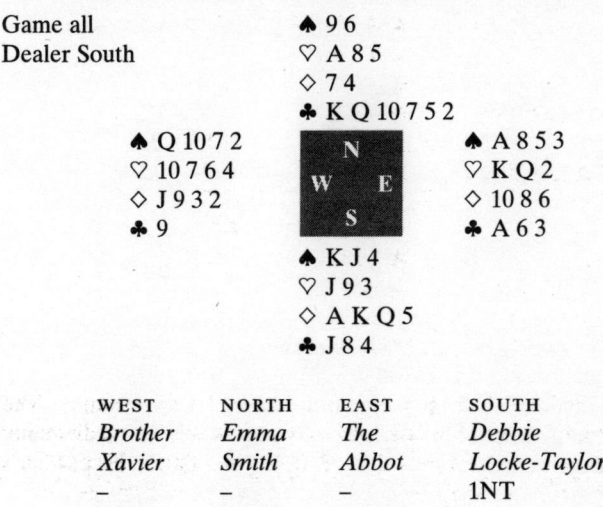

```
                    ♠ 9 6
                    ♡ A 8 5
                    ◇ 7 4
                    ♣ K Q 10 7 5 2
  ♠ Q 10 7 2                        ♠ A 8 5 3
  ♡ 10 7 6 4          N             ♡ K Q 2
  ◇ J 9 3 2        W     E          ◇ 10 8 6
  ♣ 9                 S             ♣ A 6 3
                    ♠ K J 4
                    ♡ J 9 3
                    ◇ A K Q 5
                    ♣ J 8 4
```

WEST	NORTH	EAST	SOUTH
Brother	*Emma*	*The*	*Debbie*
Xavier	*Smith*	*Abbot*	*Locke-Taylor*
–	–	–	1NT
Pass	3NT	All Pass	

North raised her partner's 15-17 point 1NT opening to game and Brother Xavier launched the defence with the two of spades. The Abbot won with the ace and paused to consider his next move.

Brother Xavier could hold at most three points, so it was not possible for him to hold K-J-x-x in the spade suit. The risk of continuing with a spade was evident. Declarer might win with the king and clear the club suit. Holding up the club ace for a round or two would then be of no use because the ace of hearts would serve as an entry.

The Abbot nodded thoughtfully. Had Brother Xavier or any of these students been sitting East, they would no doubt have let the contract through already by returning a spade. To a Grandmaster such as himself, the right defence was as spectacular as it was obvious. He must switch to the king of hearts, to drive out the ace! He would then be able to hold up the ace of clubs and cut declarer off from the dummy.

At Trick 2 the Abbot switched to the king of hearts, which was allowed to win. He lost no time in continuing with the queen of hearts and declarer won in the dummy. She played a club to the jack and a second club to dummy's king, West discarding a heart. The Abbot had to duck the second round of clubs and these cards remained:

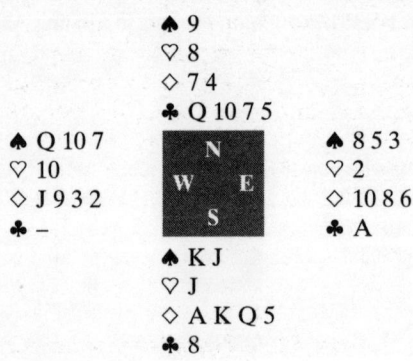

```
                    ♠ 9
                    ♡ 8
                    ◇ 7 4
                    ♣ Q 10 7 5
    ♠ Q 10 7                      ♠ 8 5 3
    ♡ 10          N              ♡ 2
    ◇ J 9 3 2    W   E           ◇ 10 8 6
    ♣ –              S           ♣ A
                    ♠ K J
                    ♡ J
                    ◇ A K Q 5
                    ♣ 8
```

Debbie Locke-Taylor could see that there was no point in clearing the club suit. Instead she played a heart to the jack, followed by three rounds of diamonds. She then exited in diamonds, throwing Brother Xavier on lead. A spade into the K-J tenace gave her a ninth trick and the game was made.

'Not the best defence, Abbot,' observed Brother Xavier. 'The king of hearts switch was good but when that won you needed to switch back to spades.'

The student declarer nodded. 'You make three spades, one heart and one club,' she said.

His head spinning, the Abbot returned his cards to the wallet. Had he defended too quickly? At the time it had seemed obvious to continue the assault on dummy's ace of hearts. Any further discussion on the board was interrupted by a loud knock on the cardroom door. Welcoming this distraction, the Abbot rose to his feet and strode towards the door. He opened it to find some half a dozen novices gazing innocently at him.

'Yes?' boomed the Abbot.

'We wondered if we might watch a few hands of your match, Abbot,' said Brother Damien, who had been appointed as spokesman. 'It would be such a valuable experience for us to see how you and Brother Xavier bid and play the cards.'

The Abbot stepped out into the corridor, where his words could not be overheard by the other players. 'Why didn't you come to watch our Hampshire League match against the Catchpole team last week?' he demanded. 'By an amazing coincidence this sudden thirst for knowledge just happens to have arisen when the opponents are some inadequately clad young girls.'

'Are they, Abbot?' said Brother Adam, whose voice was yet to break. 'We didn't know who you were playing against, actually. We just wanted to watch so we could improve our bridge.'

'Don't be so absurd!' exclaimed the Abbot. 'If you have no duties to perform, you can report to Brother Zac. I'm sure he will find you something useful to do.'

Closing the door firmly behind him, the Abbot returned to his seat. He smiled at the two young opponents in turn. 'That play I made on the last board is known as a Merrimac Coup,' he informed them. 'It may have failed unluckily on this occasion but . . . well, it's one for you both to remember!'

11.   The Abbot's Safe Lead

With eight boards to play in their second-round Hampshire Knock-out match, the monastery team was losing by 29 IMPs to the all-girl team from Southampton University.

'Can you imagine the hilarity in the novitiate if we lose this one?' thundered the Abbot. 'They'll tell the story for decades . . . making out that it was all my fault, no doubt.'

They wouldn't be far wrong in that respect, thought Brother Lucius. 'These youngsters play a strong game,' he replied. 'It's not easy to see where 29 IMPs will come from.'

The Abbot peered over his glasses at Brother Lucius. 'We can do without that sort of defeatist attitude,' he retorted. 'I expect every member of the team to give of his best.'

The final set began and this was the first board at the Abbot's table:

Game all
Dealer West

```
                    ♠ A J 10 2
                    ♡ A K Q 6 3
                    ◇ K Q 6 4
                    ♣ —
    ♠ 9 7 4                           ♠ 8 6
    ♡ 9                 N             ♡ J 10 8 2
    ◇ J 3          W         E        ◇ 10 9 5 2
    ♣ A K Q J 10 9 2        S        ♣ 7 6 3
                    ♠ K Q 5 3
                    ♡ 7 5 4
                    ◇ A 8 7
                    ♣ 8 5 4
```

WEST	NORTH	EAST	SOUTH
The	*Emma*	*Brother*	*Debbie*
Abbot	*Smith*	*Xavier*	*Locke-Taylor*
3NT	4♣	Pass	4♠
Pass	5♣	Pass	5◇
Pass	5NT	Pass	7♠
All Pass			

'What did Four Clubs mean?' queried the Abbot, who was on lead.

'Normal,' Debbie Locke-Taylor replied. 'Club shortage with emphasis on the majors.'

The Abbot, who had played the game for forty years without ever discussing a defence to the Acol 3NT, led a top club against the grand slam. Debbie Locke-Taylor ruffed in the dummy, cashed the ace of trumps and returned to her hand by overtaking the jack of trumps with the king. When trumps proved to be 3-2 she ruffed a second club in the dummy. A diamond to the ace allowed her to draw the last trump and she discarded a diamond from dummy. Three rounds of hearts revealed a 4-1 break but this caused no problem. She ruffed a heart in her hand and returned to dummy with a diamond. The grand slam had been made.

With a sigh the Abbot returned his cards to the wallet. Thirteen tricks had been trivially easy. If Lucius and Paulo missed the grand they would have no excuse at all – not with thirteen tricks on top.

'Unfortunate lead, Abbot,' observed Brother Xavier. 'Declarer was short of entries to her hand. If you lead a trump, I don't think she can ruff two clubs.'

Debbie Locke-Taylor nodded in agreement, the light catching her chestnut-brown hair. 'A red-suit lead would beat it too,' she said. 'The club lead was the only one to let it through.'

Emma Smith smiled sympathetically at the Abbot. 'You should have come to one of our lectures last Thursday,' she said. 'You could have sat next to me.'

'One of your lectures?' grunted the Abbot. 'What on earth are you talking about?'

'We're all on the new Bridge Studies course at Southampton University,' the girl replied. 'The best lecture of the week is on Thursday afternoon, given by a local Grandmaster. Do you know someone called David Hoggitt?'

'Hoggitt? Of course we do,' the Abbot replied. 'We play against him every year in the County League.'

'He gives away all the expert's secrets,' continued Emma Smith excitedly. 'On Thursday he told us that you should always lead a trump against a grand slam.'

The Abbot's mouth fell open. 'Hoggitt knows almost nothing about opening leads,' he declared. 'In any case the recommendation to lead a trump against a grand is simply because it's safe. Nothing could be safer than a top card from a solid side suit.'

Emma Smith made a note of the Abbot's hand on the back of her scorecard. 'David and I usually have coffee together after his lecture,' she said. 'I'll ask him what he would have led from your hand.'

Brother Xavier somehow maintained a straight face. How Lucius and Paulo would enjoy his account of this exchange afterwards!

Lucius and Paulo, meanwhile, were doing their best to reduce the gap. This hand had just been dealt:

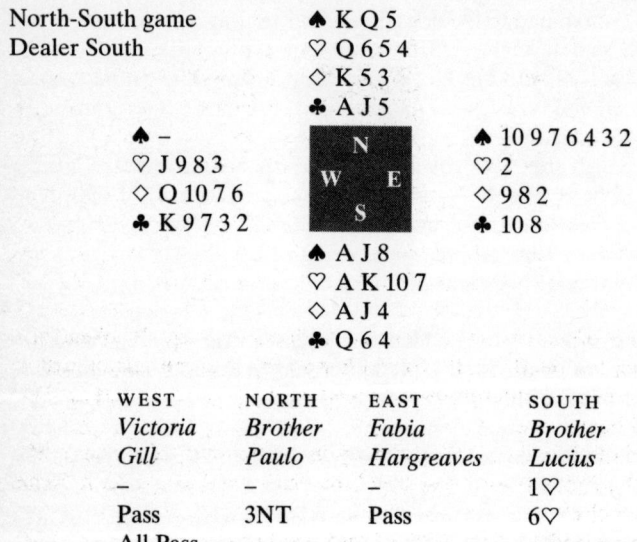

North-South game
Dealer South

♠ K Q 5
♡ Q 6 5 4
◇ K 5 3
♣ A J 5

♠ –
♡ J 9 8 3
◇ Q 10 7 6
♣ K 9 7 3 2

♠ 10 9 7 6 4 3 2
♡ 2
◇ 9 8 2
♣ 10 8

♠ A J 8
♡ A K 10 7
◇ A J 4
♣ Q 6 4

WEST	NORTH	EAST	SOUTH
Victoria	*Brother*	*Fabia*	*Brother*
Gill	*Paulo*	*Hargreaves*	*Lucius*
–	–	–	1♡
Pass	3NT	Pass	6♡
All Pass			

Brother Paulo's 3NT response showed a sound raise to the heart game. Brother Lucius thumbed through his cards uncertainly. The nineteen high-card points suggested a slam. Against that, he had a full seven losers in his hand. Still, surely the moment had come to make some inroads into the 29-IMP deficit. He rebid 6♡, ending the auction, and the six of diamonds was led.

Brother Lucius captured East's eight of diamonds with the jack and continued with the ace and queen of trumps, East showing out. Since West was marked with the diamond queen, Lucius knew that it was safe to return to his hand in that suit. His next move was a finesse of the jack of clubs, which proved successful. He gave a small nod, to let Paulo know that the slam was assured, and then played the king of trumps followed by the last diamond winner.

When Lucius turned to the spade suit Victoria Gill was disinclined to ruff with her master trump. If she did, she would have to lead away from the ♣K or play her last diamond, conceding a ruff-and-discard. She discarded a club on the first round of spades and another on the second. These cards remained:

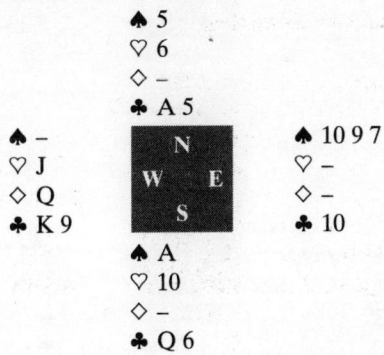

```
              ♠ 5
              ♡ 6
              ◇ –
              ♣ A 5
  ♠ –                      ♠ 10 9 7
  ♡ J        N             ♡ –
  ◇ Q    W       E         ◇ –
  ♣ K 9      S             ♣ 10
              ♠ A
              ♡ 10
              ◇ –
              ♣ Q 6
```

When Brother Lucius persevered with another spade, West discarded her last diamond. It brought her no relief. Lucius exited with a trump to the jack and ran the enforced club return to his queen. The slam had been made.

Victoria Gill looked apologetically in her partner's direction. 'My opening lead didn't work very well,' she observed. 'Is it better if I lead something else?'

'All three leads give me a trick,' said Brother Lucius. 'A trump lead makes it slightly more difficult. I can end-play you in the minors if I read the cards right.'

Back at the other table the Abbot was feeling distinctly weary. The final set had not gone well for him. Still, if he could conjure a big swing on this final board and Lucius and Paulo produced a strong card from the other table, the match might still be won. Miracles did happen – or so someone in his position was meant to believe.

This was the last board of the match:

Love all
Dealer South

```
                    ♠ Q 9 7 5 3
                    ♡ 3
                    ◇ 7 3
                    ♣ A K Q J 8
    ♠ K J 10 6 4         N           ♠ 8
    ♡ K Q J 8 5      W       E       ♡ 9 7 6 2
    ◇ 9 8 5              S           ◇ J 10 6 4
    ♣ —                             ♣ 10 7 3 2
                    ♠ A 2
                    ♡ A 10 4
                    ◇ A K Q 2
                    ♣ 9 6 5 4
```

WEST	NORTH	EAST	SOUTH
The	*Emma*	*Brother*	*Debbie*
Abbot	*Smith*	*Xavier*	*Locke-Taylor*
–	–	–	1♣
2♣	3♡	Pass	3♠
Pass	5♣	Pass	6♣
All Pass			

The Abbot entered the auction with a Michaels cue bid, showing both majors, and Emma Smith's 3♡ was a splinter bid with clubs agreed as trumps. Debbie Locke-Taylor placed her partner with good trumps when she heard a jump to the club game. She bid a sixth club on the strength of her excellent controls and the king of hearts was led.

'I don't know if these will be any use,' said Emma Smith, grinning as she laid out her splendid trump holding. 'Nothing much else, I'm afraid.'

'Very nice, Emma,' her partner replied. 'Small, please.'

Declarer won with the heart ace and led a trump from the South hand. An easy contract suddenly became difficult when West showed out, discarding a heart. It would not now be possible to ruff a spade in the South hand. Nor could declarer take more than one ruff in the dummy, without promoting East's ♣10 into the setting trick.

Debbie Locke-Taylor could see a different chance. She drew all four rounds of trumps and then turned to the diamond suit. As she had foreseen, the Abbot was soon under pressure. This was the position with one top diamond still to be played:

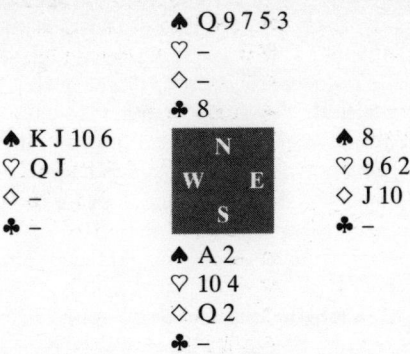

```
              ♠ Q 9 7 5 3
              ♡ —
              ◇ —
              ♣ 8
♠ K J 10 6                    ♠ 8
♡ Q J          N              ♡ 9 6 2
◇ —          W   E            ◇ J 10
♣ —            S              ♣ —
              ♠ A 2
              ♡ 10 4
              ◇ Q 2
              ♣ —
```

Debbie Locke-Taylor led the diamond queen and turned to survey the Abbot with her dark brown eyes. The Abbot had no good card to play. If he threw the ♠6, ace and another spade would set up two winners in the dummy. When he eventually threw the ♡J instead, the young declarer led the ♡4 to the next trick, driving out the Abbot's queen. Not only did this set up her ♡10 as an eleventh trick, it also forced the Abbot to concede a twelfth trick by leading away from the spade king. The slam had been made.

It seemed that Debbie Locke-Taylor did not regard her excellent piece of dummy play as anything out of the ordinary. 'They'll probably bid it at the other table too,' she observed. 'With 29 IMPs to make up, they'll be punting everything.'

The Abbot could not believe what he was hearing. It was totally inappropriate for young players to display such confidence at the table, particularly if they were female. Did they not realise they were facing opponents of the highest calibre? Anyone with more experience of the game would be quaking in their shoes, making mistakes all over the place. He looked across to the far side of the card room, where the other table had also finished play. 'Let's go, Xavier,' he said.

'We may have done enough,' said Brother Lucius as the Abbot arrived. 'Three big ones and some useful part-scores.'

Brother Xavier dispelled this notion with a shake of the head and the final comparison did indeed reveal a loss by 21 IMPs. Dispatching his scorecard to a nearby wastepaper basket, the Abbot rose dutifully to his feet. The underclad female visitors would have to be carefully ushered from the Monastery, away from the prying eyes of any novices who might still be up. He'd better check that the coast was clear.

The Abbot opened the cardroom door and could not believe the sight before him. Brother Zac was polishing an old table that had remained unpolished for decades. A group of around ten novices were standing further down the corridor. Brother Fabius and Brother Michael were repairing the skirting board and the ancient Brother Wilfred had been brought from the infirmary in his wheel chair. As he had informed the monastery doctor, this might be his last chance to see four attractive young females.

'What on earth are you all doing here at this time of night?' demanded the Abbot.

'This table has been looking dull for ages,' replied Brother Zac.

'And this loose skirting board has become very dangerous,' added Brother Fabius.

'Did you win your match, Abbot?' asked Brother Cameron. 'We wanted to hear the result.'

'Go to your cells immediately, all of you!' exclaimed the Abbot. 'I've never witnessed such disgraceful behaviour.'

The Abbot returned to the cardroom, closing the door behind him. 'A small problem outside,' he declared. 'It will soon be dealt with.' He smiled broadly at the four girls. 'Now, you must join us for a small drink before you leave,' he said. 'Get that bottle of Brother Anthony's elderflower champagne from the Buttery fridge, will you, Xavier? Nothing but the best for these charming young ladies!'

12.   Brother Aelred's Glimpse of Heaven

The Abbot peered closely at the elderly Brother Fabius, as he took his seat. 'Are you growing a beard?' he demanded.

Brother Fabius nodded happily and gave the emerging white hairs a stroke. 'I thought I should show solidarity with my partner,' he replied. 'Not that my beard is ever likely to rival Brother Zac's.'

The Abbot shook his head in disbelief. Did Fabius realise how ridiculous he looked? People wore beards for only three reasons – to cover their face if they were shy, to hide a feeble chin, or to attempt to draw attention from their baldness. None of these excuses applied to Brother Fabius, so why on earth choose, voluntarily, to look as absurd as that?

The players drew their cards for this board:

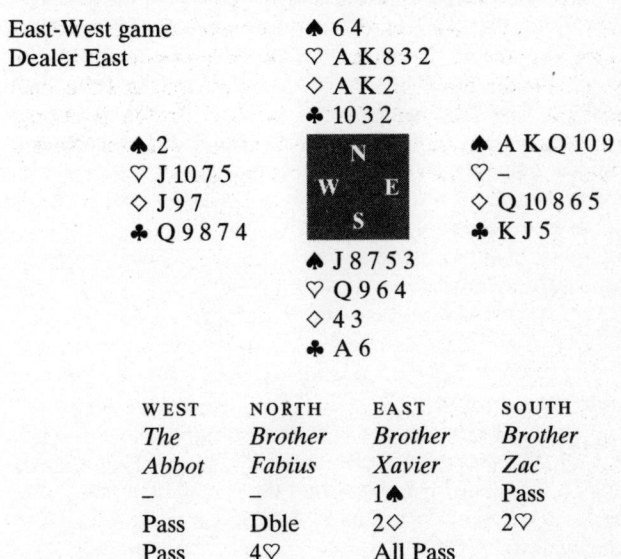

East-West game
Dealer East

```
                    ♠ 6 4
                    ♡ A K 8 3 2
                    ◇ A K 2
                    ♣ 10 3 2
    ♠ 2                          ♠ A K Q 10 9
    ♡ J 10 7 5          N        ♡ –
    ◇ J 9 7         W     E      ◇ Q 10 8 6 5
    ♣ Q 9 8 7 4        S         ♣ K J 5
                    ♠ J 8 7 5 3
                    ♡ Q 9 6 4
                    ◇ 4 3
                    ♣ A 6
```

WEST	NORTH	EAST	SOUTH
The	*Brother*	*Brother*	*Brother*
Abbot	*Fabius*	*Xavier*	*Zac*
–	–	1♠	Pass
Pass	Dble	2◇	2♡
Pass	4♡	All Pass	

The Abbot was not overjoyed to see Brother Zac at the helm of the first contract. Zac was known as a fair card-player, whereas Fabius had little idea of the game. Was there any law against Brother Fabius playing a hand or two against him? The Abbot led his singleton spade and down went the dummy, with its five-card heart suit.

'Why didn't you bid Two Hearts on that?' demanded the Abbot. 'You would have played the hand, then.'

'I was in the protective seat,' replied Brother Fabius.

'Yes, yes I realise that,' grunted the Abbot. 'So what?'

Brother Fabius assumed a learned expression. 'In the protective seat we play the Rule of the Transferred King,' he continued. 'Add a king to my hand and I have 17 points. That's too strong for an overcall of Two Hearts.'

'It certainly is,' agreed Brother Zac. 'Particularly in the protective seat.'

Brother Xavier won the opening lead with the spade queen and cashed the ace of spades, the Abbot throwing a diamond. The diamond switch was won with dummy's ace and Brother Zac then cashed the king of diamonds. When everyone followed, he made the strange move of continuing with a third diamond, throwing a club loser from his hand.

On lead with the diamond queen, Brother Xavier tried his luck with a club switch. Declarer won with the ace and played the queen of trumps, East showing out. 'I have the rest now,' he said, turning towards the Abbot. 'I can play a second trump, covering your card, and then cross-ruff the remainder.'

With a pained expression the Abbot returned his cards to the wallet. It was a pity that Fabius hadn't played the contract. The chance of him making ten tricks with the trumps 4-1 was as remote as that of his beard ever looking impressive. Had Zac known what he was doing? The loser-on-loser play was quite a smart move. Without it he would have run into a trump promotion.

Brother Fabius nodded wisely as he inspected the traveller. 'Yes, the heart game goes down, played by North,' he observed. 'It's surprising how many people don't play the "transferred king" method. It brings us quite a few good results.'

A couple of rounds later, Lucius and Paulo arrived at the Abbot's table. 'That Brother Aelred is quite unbelievable,' said an amused Brother Lucius, taking his seat. 'He forgot there was still a trump out. Then, when I ruffed one of his winners, he said I must have revoked when he drew the trumps.'

Brother Paulo laughed. 'Apparently, two rounds of trumps are sufficient nowadays when you are in a 5-3 fit!'

The Abbot showed no sign of sharing in the amusement. 'Brother Aelred always manages to draw trumps against me,' he declared sourly. 'No doubt he will perform some masterful play when he comes to our table.'

A few moments later, Brother Paulo had arrived in a slam.

North-South game
Dealer West

♠ K J 8 5 3
♡ A
♢ A Q 7 5 4
♣ K 10

♠ 10 9
♡ K J 10 8 5 4
♢ J 3
♣ Q 7 4

```
    N
 W     E
    S
```

♠ 2
♡ Q 9 3
♢ K 10 9 6 2
♣ J 9 8 2

♠ A Q 7 6 4
♡ 7 6 2
♢ 8
♣ A 6 5 3

WEST	NORTH	EAST	SOUTH
Brother	*Brother*	*The*	*Brother*
Xavier	*Lucius*	*Abbot*	*Paulo*
2♡	Dble	4♡	5♠
Pass	7♠	All Pass	

Brother Xavier led the ten of trumps against the grand slam in spades and Lucius displayed his dummy. 'Sorry if we're missing an ace, Paulo,' he said. 'It was a bit of a pot, bidding seven.'

'Very suitable hand,' the Italian replied.

Brother Paulo surveyed the dummy thoughtfully. If West ♠10 was a singleton, a crossruff stood a good chance of succeeding. A singleton trump was rather a risky lead, though, particularly as a heart lead was likely to be safe. The Abbot would need a bit of shape for his double raise, too. Surely it was East who held the singleton trump. In that case it would be better to draw the outstanding trump and play to set up dummy's diamond suit.

Brother Paulo drew a second round of trumps, pleased to see that it was indeed West who produced the last trump. He cashed the two red aces and ruffed a diamond. A heart ruff was followed by a second diamond ruff, West showing out.

'I'm pleased to see that the suits don't *always* break evenly for you,' observed the Abbot.

'I may still be all right, I think,' declared the Italian. 'I have another ball in my locker, as you English say.'

This position had been reached:

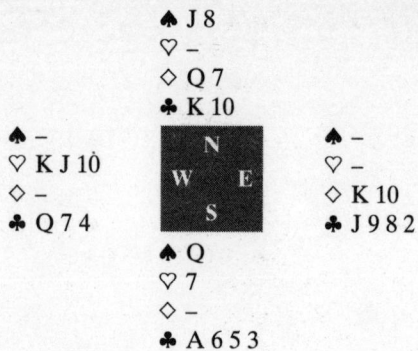

                    ♠ J 8
                    ♡ –
                    ◇ Q 7
                    ♣ K 10

    ♠ –   ♠ –
    ♡ K J 10   ♡ –
    ◇ –   ◇ K 10
    ♣ Q 7 4   ♣ J 9 8 2

                    ♠ Q
                    ♡ 7
                    ◇ –
                    ♣ A 6 5 3

Brother Paulo ruffed his last heart in dummy and turned to observe the Abbot, who still had a discard to make. 'You are two-four in the minors, no?' he said. 'I can ruff a trick good in whichever suit you will throw.'

The Abbot discarded a club and Brother Paulo proceeded to ruff a trick good in the club suit. The grand slam was his.

Brother Lucius smiled as he inspected the scoresheet. 'Only one pair managed to reach the *small* slam,' he announced. 'There was no need for me to take such a risk.'

'No, it was good grand,' Paulo replied. 'If the pre-empter has one trump, a cross-ruff is easy.'

'Does a club lead cause any problem?' enquired Brother Xavier.

'No, no, I didn't need the club king as an entry,' the Italian replied. 'It was easy on any lead.'

Quite so, thought the Abbot. When two pairs of their calibre faced each other, the top on this board would go to whoever was lucky enough to be sitting North-South.

A couple of rounds later, the Abbot's mood was improved by the arrival of some welcome visitors.

'We all make mistakes,' said Brother Aelred, taking his seat, 'but it shouldn't be too difficult to return partner's suit, particularly in no-trumps. I had four spade tricks to take!'

'I was put off by your lead of the nine,' said Brother Michael. 'I'm not sure that's the right card from A-Q-10-9-x.'

'I led my fourth-best card to make it absolutely clear to you,' continued Brother Aelred. 'If I lead the ten, you might think my suit was ten-high.'

'Entertaining as your conversation is,' intervened the Abbot, 'we do have two boards to play.'

The players leaned forward to extract their cards for this deal:

Game all   ♠ K J
Dealer East   ♡ 9 5 2
                    ◇ J 10 4
                    ♣ A Q 9 4 2

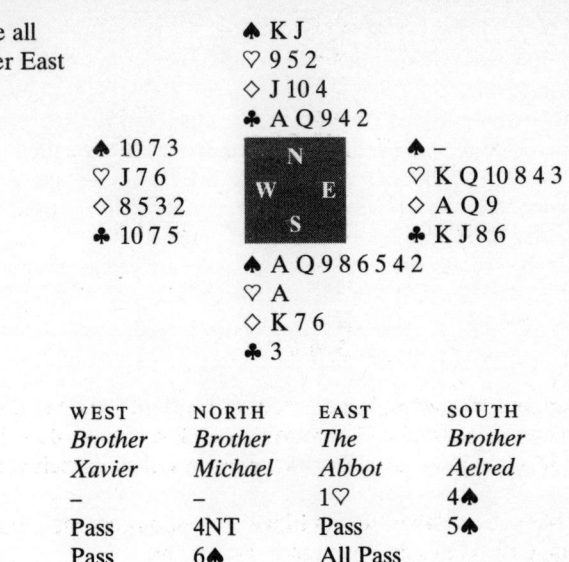

   ♠ 10 7 3   ♠ –
   ♡ J 7 6   ♡ K Q 10 8 4 3
   ◇ 8 5 3 2   ◇ A Q 9
   ♣ 10 7 5   ♣ K J 8 6

                    ♠ A Q 9 8 6 5 4 2
                    ♡ A
                    ◇ K 7 6
                    ♣ 3

WEST	NORTH	EAST	SOUTH
Brother	*Brother*	*The*	*Brother*
Xavier	*Michael*	*Abbot*	*Aelred*
–	–	1♡	4♠
Pass	4NT	Pass	5♠
Pass	6♠	All Pass	

Brother Aelred arrived in Six Spades and the six of hearts was led.

'I have an opening bid for you, partner!' announced Brother Michael. 'I had to make one slam try after your jump.'

The Abbot stared in disbelief at the dummy's heart holding. 'You had nowhere near enough to bid on over Four Spades,' he declared. 'You might have had two heart losers, for one thing.'

'I don't think Aelred would jump to the four-level with two heart losers,' replied Brother Michael. 'Anyway, I was hoping he had the ace of hearts. That's why I bid 4NT.'

'Good bid, partner,' said Brother Aelred. 'I do have the ace of hearts, as it happens.'

For a brief moment the Abbot closed his eyes. Would it not be possible, just once, for Aelred to have the ace of diamonds and a couple of heart losers? Was that too difficult for Him Up There to arrange? If Brother Aelred always held the right ace, they would go on mis-using Blackwood all their lives.

Brother Aelred won the first trick with the heart ace and drew two rounds of trumps with the king and jack. 'Small diamond,' he said.

The Abbot considered the situation carefully. Declarer had clearly started with a singleton ♡A. What did he have in diamonds? If he had three diamonds to the king, rising with the ace now would be a disaster. It would set up a finesse against the queen. If declarer held a doubleton king of diamonds, he would hold two clubs and would surely then take a club finesse. What if declarer held a singleton king of diamonds? He would then hold three clubs and would lose two tricks in that suit anyway.

The Abbot contributed the nine of diamonds to the trick. Brother Aelred won with the king and concluded that all now depended on the club finesse. The odds were against it, with East having opened, but some chance was better than none. He might as well run the trumps first, to look as if he had some clever plan in mind.

Brother Aelred ran the trump suit and soon arrived at this ending:

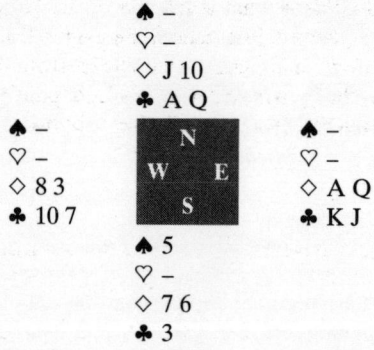

On the last trump Brother Aelred threw a diamond from dummy. The Abbot was alert to the situation. If he discarded the diamond queen, any competent declarer would throw him in with the ace of diamonds. Even Brother Aelred might be inspired enough to find the play. Should he throw the jack of clubs instead? No, a simple fellow like Aelred was bound to conclude that the king was then bare. The best way to deter a throw-in was surely to throw the ace of diamonds.

Brother Aelred was on the point of taking the club finesse when he noticed that the diamond ace had been discarded. Good gracious, had the Abbot been squeezed? If he had been forced to throw all his top diamonds, dummy's jack would be good!

Brother Aelred struggled to recall which cards had gone. He couldn't actually remember seeing the queen of diamonds but, of course, since the contract depended solely on the club finesse there had been no point in watching what cards were thrown. Let's look at it mathematically, he thought. The chance that the diamond queen was still out must be around 50%. The chance that the club finesse would work was much less than that, because the Abbot opened the bidding.

Hoping for the best, Brother Aelred led a diamond to the jack. He gave a resigned shrug of the shoulders when the jack lost to the queen. It was typical of the Abbot to throw the ace away, making him think the jack was good. Still, bridge was a cut-throat game and the Abbot was fully entitled to take advantage of a weaker player such as himself.

'The last two are yours,' grunted the Abbot. 'I have to lead a club into the tenace.'

'A brilliant strip squeeze!' congratulated Brother Xavier. 'Don't you agree, Abbot? A very fine effort.'

Brother Aelred surveyed the scene ecstatically, as if bathed in some heavenly light. So, this is what it felt like to be Brother Lucius. The Abbot had been squeezed, just as he had imagined! For just about the first time in his life he had planned a contract from beginning to end, coming up with the goods. Brother Aelred paused to savour the moment. Yes, indeed. It made all those bottoms over the years worthwhile.

13.   The Abbot's Careful Defence

The Abbot had reached the rank of Grandmaster many years ago but he was still an avid collector of green national masterpoints. 'Last year we won five matches out of seven,' he recalled, as he headed his ancient Morris Minor in the direction of a Winchester Green-point Swiss event. 'That's one and a quarter greens.'

Brother Xavier and Brother Paulo, who were sitting in the back of the car, exchanged a smile. The Abbot's attitude to green points was truly amazing. What value could they be when you had already achieved the highest ranking possible?

'If you come in the top four positions there are extra greens awarded,' continued the Abbot, crunching into first gear as his car struggled to mount a steep hill. 'No reason at all why we shouldn't manage that. The field is very moderate in these Swiss events.'

Play started at one o'clock and the Abbot was not overjoyed to face another Grandmaster, David Hoggitt, in the first round. 'Absurd that we should play each other,' he declared. 'We must be the two strongest teams here.'

'I'm not sure you're right about that,' Hoggitt replied. 'There are several teams here from other counties.'

'Second-rate green point gatherers,' declared the Abbot. 'You and I play solely to support the county, of course. Entirely different.'

This was the third board of the match:

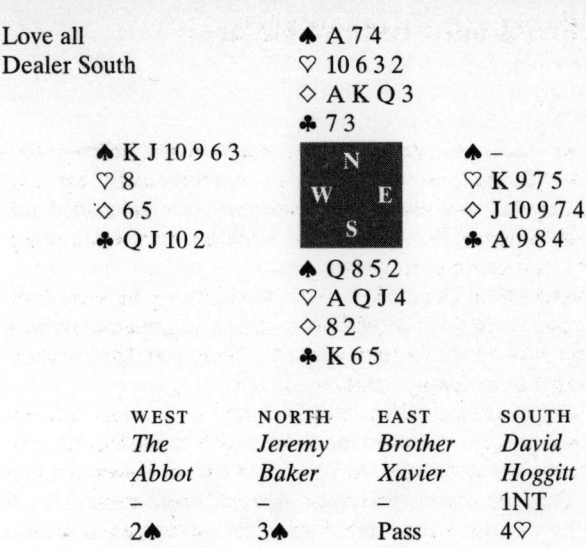

Love all
Dealer South

	♠ A 7 4
	♡ 10 6 3 2
	◇ A K Q 3
	♣ 7 3

♠ K J 10 9 6 3
♡ 8
◇ 6 5
♣ Q J 10 2

♠ –
♡ K 9 7 5
◇ J 10 9 7 4
♣ A 9 8 4

♠ Q 8 5 2
♡ A Q J 4
◇ 8 2
♣ K 6 5

WEST	NORTH	EAST	SOUTH
The	*Jeremy*	*Brother*	*David*
Abbot	*Baker*	*Xavier*	*Hoggitt*
–	–	–	1NT
2♠	3♠	Pass	4♡
All Pass			

North's response was part of the Lebensohl convention and, in the variation being played, showed both four hearts and a spade stopper. Hoggitt chose to play in hearts and the ♣Q was led.

Brother Xavier won the club lead with the ace and switched to the ◇J, won in the dummy. A trump to the queen won the next trick and declarer re-entered dummy by cashing the ♣K and ruffing a club. When a heart was played to the jack West discarded a spade. Two more rounds of diamonds left these cards still out:

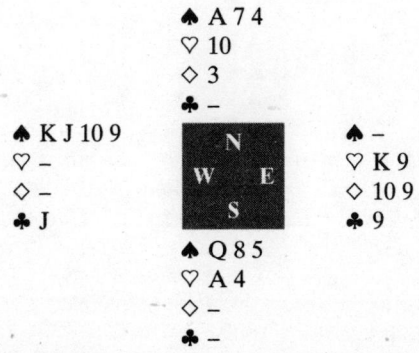

	♠ A 7 4
	♡ 10
	◇ 3
	♣ –

♠ K J 10 9
♡ –
◇ –
♣ J

♠ –
♡ K 9
◇ 10 9
♣ 9

♠ Q 8 5
♡ A 4
◇ –
♣ –

Hoggitt paused to assess the situation. By playing dummy's last diamond he could assure himself of two more tricks in the trump suit. He would not make the contract, however, since he would never make a spade trick. 'Play a low spade,' he instructed.

It could serve no purpose to ruff a loser, so Brother Xavier threw his last club. Declarer played a low spade and the Abbot won with the nine. There was nothing he could do. If he played a spade from the king, East would score just one trump trick whether he ruffed at this stage or not. The Abbot eventually decided to try his luck with a club. 'Ruff with the ten,' said Hoggitt.

Brother Xavier gave a resigned shake of the head. If he discarded, declarer would lead dummy's last diamond to promote an extra trump trick. He overruffed instead but Hoggitt simply discarded his last spade loser. The remaining three tricks were his.

With a sigh the Abbot returned his cards to the wallet. Apart from himself, Hoggitt was probably the only declarer in the field good enough to make such a tricky contract. Ah well, there was no point bemoaning the absurd first-round draw. Perhaps Lucius or Paulo would fall into the right line.

A couple of deals later Hoggitt arrived in a slam.

North-South game
Dealer South

	♠ A K 6		
	♡ 10 4 2		
	◇ Q 7 5 4		
	♣ J 7 4		
♠ Q J 10 8 5 4 2		♠ 9 7	
♡ –		♡ Q 9 8 6	
◇ 10 3		◇ A J 9 6 2	
♣ 10 8 6 5		♣ 9 2	
	♠ 3		
	♡ A K J 7 5 3		
	◇ K 8		
	♣ A K Q 3		

WEST	NORTH	EAST	SOUTH
The	*Jeremy*	*Brother*	*David*
Abbot	*Baker*	*Xavier*	*Hoggitt*
–	–	–	2♡
3♠	4♡	Pass	4NT
Pass	5◇	Pass	6♡
All Pass			

Hoggitt opened with an Acol two-bid and the Abbot attempted to make life awkward for his opponents with a 3♠ overcall. When they reached a small slam in hearts he led the queen of spades, won in the dummy.

With spades likely to be divided 7-2, East was a strong favourite to hold the queen of trumps. 'Play the ten of trumps,' said Hoggitt.

The card was covered by the queen and ace, West discarding a spade. Hoggitt saw that he could pick up East's remaining 9-8-6 in the trump suit, provided he could arrange two more entries to the dummy. The jack of clubs was good for one entry. If the defenders made the mistake of capturing the king of diamonds, the diamond queen would serve as a second entry. Hoggitt adjusted his glasses. Wait a moment! Suppose the defenders did hold up the ace of diamonds when he played the king. He could then cross to the jack of clubs and throw his other diamond on the king of spades.

When Hoggitt played the king of diamonds from his hand, the Abbot signalled his count with the ten and Brother Xavier won with the ace. His club return ran to dummy's jack and Hoggitt called for a trump. After capturing East's nine with the jack, Hoggitt re-entered dummy with the diamond queen and led a third round of trumps. A marked finesse of the seven picked up the suit and the small slam had been made.

'I don't believe it!' cried the Abbot.

Several players from adjacent tables looked over. 'Shh!' said a large woman in a floral dress.

'I gave you the right count signal in diamonds,' continued the Abbot loudly. 'Hold up the diamond ace, for Heaven's sake! That kills the entry to dummy.'

Hoggitt sat quietly, enjoying the moment to the full. There was no hurry to point out that this defence would not work. The Abbot was a pompous old fool at the best of times. It would serve him right if he made an exhibition of himself.

'Hold up the diamond ace?' said Brother Xavier. 'Does that beat it?'

'Am I playing with a complete idiot?' exclaimed the Abbot. 'Of course it beats it! You can explain this one to the others.'

'If you can't keep quiet, I'm going to call the Director,' said the floral-dressed woman. 'We're trying to concentrate here.'

Brother Xavier leaned forward, reducing his voice to a whisper. 'I was worried that he'd be able to throw his other diamond away,' he said. 'If you had seven spades, he would have a discard on dummy's king.'

The Abbot turned towards Hoggitt. 'Is that right?' he said.

Hoggitt looked back impassively. 'Yes, twelve tricks were cold,' he said.

'What about on a diamond lead?' persisted the Abbot. 'If you double the 5◇ Blackwood response, Xavier, I would lead a diamond.'

'It makes no difference,' said Hoggitt. 'Your partner has to take the diamond ace or I can discard my other diamond. I unblock the king from my hand and again I have three entries to dummy to pick up the trumps.'

'Our only chance is if you don't overcall,' observed Brother Xavier. 'Then he'd have no reason to finesse in trumps.'

The match was soon over and the monastery team found that they had lost by 14 Victory Points to 6. 'Very disappointing,' declared the Abbot. 'Even against a reasonably strong team I had hoped we might start with a win.'

Brother Paulo looked down at his own scorecard – seven healthy plus scores and just a 110 in the minus column. He too had been expecting a win. 'We were a bit unlucky, perhaps,' he said. 'At least now we should play a weak team.'

Brother Paulo's expectations were proved incorrect when the Abbot found himself facing Professor Deakin on the next round. A scientist of international repute, he was a wild and unpredictable bidder.

'You lost your first match, too?' enquired Professor Deakin.

'I didn't expect to,' the Abbot replied. 'Our other pair had a disappointing card.'

'Ours too,' said Deakin. 'I managed to get out for 1100 on one board, with an easy vulnerable slam the other way. Our other pair stopped in game.'

'It wasn't an easy slam to bid, John,' his partner observed. 'They only had 22 points between them.'

'We'd have bid it,' replied Deakin. 'It was Steve's fault for not opening.'

A couple of part-scores were followed by the first big board of the set:

Game all · ♠ K
Dealer South · ♡ 10 4 3
· ♢ Q 10 9 8 6 5 4 2
· ♣ 10

```
♠ J 9 8 5 4 2          N          ♠ A 7 6 3
♡ K 2               W     E        ♡ A 9 8 6
♢ J 7                  S           ♢ –
♣ K 9 3                            ♣ A J 7 6 2
```

· ♠ Q 10
· ♡ Q J 7 5
· ♢ A K 3
· ♣ Q 8 5 4

WEST	NORTH	EAST	SOUTH
Brother	*Prof*	*The*	*Julian*
Xavier	*Deakin*	*Abbot*	*Wells*
–	–	–	1NT
Pass	3NT	All Pass	

After a mundane-sounding auction Brother Xavier led ♠5 against 3NT. Looking pleased with himself, Professor Deakin laid out the dummy. The Abbot surveyed his opponent wearily. Five points and an eight-card diamond suit? Was Deakin a complete lunatic? His partner's 1NT opening was of the 12-14 variety and there was no reason at all to expect the diamond suit to run. If it didn't, the contract would go several hundred down.

The Abbot won dummy's ♠K with the ace, noting the ten falling on his left. It was possible that declarer had started with J-10 doubleton in spades and that the suit would run. However, no world-class defender would rely on this chance alone. The best idea was surely to lay down an ace or two. If Brother Xavier gave an encouraging signal on one of those, it might be possible to beat the contract even when declarer held the ♠Q and the diamond suit was running.

With a Grandmasterly nod of the head the Abbot led the ace of clubs to the second trick. Thinking that his nine of clubs might be too valuable a card to waste, Brother Xavier contributed the three of clubs to this trick. Continuing with his plan, the Abbot next played the ace of hearts. Brother Xavier was now in a quandary. The defenders had scored three aces and he had two cashable kings in his hand. It could serve no purpose to play the king of hearts under the ace. He would have to play the two and hope for the best.

The Abbot could sense some sort of electricity in the air but there could surely be no doubt about his continuation. Xavier had given him an unequivocal lowest spot-card in both hearts and clubs. This could only mean that he held the queen of spades and wanted a return to the spade suit. With the air of someone who had done everything humanly possible, the Abbot switched back to spades.

'Just the nine,' said Julian Wells, winning with the spade queen and claiming eight diamond tricks.

The Abbot looked anxiously across the table. 'What did you have in clubs?' he demanded.

'King-nine-one,' Brother Xavier replied. 'I didn't think I could afford to signal with the nine. It might be an important card.'

'I don't have X-ray vision!' cried the Abbot. 'I'm obviously not going to play another club if you give me the lowest spot card.'

Brother Xavier returned his cards resignedly to the wallet. 'I had the ♡K too,' he said. 'Only king-two doubleton, unfortunately, so I had to give you the two. It works better if you cash the ♡A first. Then I know that I can afford to encourage in clubs.'

'Oh, I see, it was all *my* fault,' said the Abbot heavily. 'I'm probably the only defender in the whole event who would lay down the aces rather than playing back a spade immediately. What's worse, I think we could have made Four Spades.'

'You can make Six Spades,' said Professor Deakin. 'There's no elimination play but you can cash the ♣A, dropping my 10, and then finesse the nine.' He looked across at his partner. 'I thought they'd have something big on, Julian. That's why I bid 3NT.'

His partner nodded happily. 'Nice bid, John,' he replied. 'We were unlucky that the king of spades didn't win at Trick 1.'

The Abbot groaned inwardly. One thing he couldn't stand was opponents who gloated over a good result. They'd been unlucky, did he say? Scoring +600 when the opponents were cold for a vulnerable slam was the sort of luck he wouldn't mind having himself. Xavier had a six-card spade suit. Why hadn't he overcalled? It was typical to allow himself to be outbid by a known villain such as Professor Deakin. Unless Xavier pulled himself together very quickly, that would be another quarter-green down the drain. They'd probably find themselves on one of the bottom tables, playing that obnoxious woman in the floral dress.

The Abbot sat back in his chair, surveying the scene as he waited for play to finish at the other table. The Good Lord knew what He was talking about, when it came to Sundays. A day of rest would have been far more enjoyable.

14.   Brother Xavier's Unlucky Opening Lead

The first two rounds of the Winchester Green-point Swiss had not gone to plan and the monastery team was near the tail of the field.

Elsie Bonneville, who had recently celebrated her eightieth birthday, welcomed the Abbot to Table 47. 'We always lose our first two matches in these Swiss events,' she said. 'It's only when you get down to these bottom tables that you have a reasonable chance of picking up a quarter-green.'

The Abbot stared in disbelief at his ancient opponent. Had she no idea who she was talking to? If not, she very soon would have . . . when her side had been dispatched 20-0 with a couple of dozen IMPs to spare. 'It takes longer than two rounds for the field to sort itself out,' he replied.

The match was a board or two old when Elsie Bonneville arrived in a slam.

```
Game all          ♠ K 7
Dealer South      ♡ K Q 8 3
                  ◇ A 10 6 3
                  ♣ K Q 7
    ♠ J 10 9 6        N        ♠ Q 8 5 4 3
    ♡ 6 4       W         E    ♡ 9 5
    ◇ 9 7 4                    ◇ Q J
    ♣ A 10 8 2       S        ♣ J 9 5 3
                  ♠ A 2
                  ♡ A J 10 7 2
                  ◇ K 8 5 2
                  ♣ 6 4
```

WEST	NORTH	EAST	SOUTH
Brother	*Joyce*	*The*	*Elsie*
Xavier	*Cotter*	*Abbot*	*Bonneville*
–	–	–	1♡
Pass	4NT	Pass	5♡
Pass	6♡	All Pass	

Brother Xavier led the jack of spades and down went the dummy. 'Just five losers for you, Elsie,' said Joyce Cotter, who was wearing a somewhat ugly neck brace. 'That should be enough for a slam, facing seven losers.'

'It wasn't enough on the last round,' her partner replied. 'Still I don't think I played that one to best advantage.'

Come on, come on, thought the Abbot. Had these old dears come here to talk or to play bridge?

Declarer won the jack of spades lead with the ace and drew trumps in two rounds. She then turned her mind towards the diamond suit, leaning forward to inspect the dummy's holding. Ace-ten to four, was it? It was a pity Joyce didn't have the ace-queen to four. That would have made things a bit easier. Should she play the ace first or the king? It didn't seem to make any difference, she thought, let's try the king.

The Abbot, sitting East, contributed a smooth ◇Q to the trick. Mrs Bonneville continued with a second round of diamonds, a small card appearing from West. Which card should she play from dummy? She had read somewhere that when an honour appeared from a defender, it was more likely to be a singleton than one of two touching honours. What nonsense! A 3-2 break was twice as likely as a 4-1 break. Everyone knew that. East's ◇Q was therefore twice as likely to be from ◇Q-J doubleton as to be a singleton. Mrs Bonneville pointed a confident finger at the dummy. 'Play the ace, partner,' she said.

With ill grace the Abbot spun the ◇J onto the table.

'I make twelve tricks now,' said Elsie Bonneville, facing her remaining cards. 'I'll give you the ace of clubs.'

'You guessed the diamond suit well, partner,' observed the North player. 'If the queen was a singleton, you could have finessed the ten on the second round.'

'Some people say you should finesse,' Elsie Bonneville replied. 'It's absolute rubbish, as this hand proves. In any case, he looked as if he had the jack.'

The Abbot sat back in his chair, gritting his teeth. Silly old bat! What good would finessing the ten have been, even if his queen had been a singleton? With four diamonds in both hands she would still have had a diamond loser.

'Could be a bad one for us,' said Brother Xavier. 'Lucius or Paulo may play on clubs first. With a discard coming on the clubs you can afford to follow Restricted Choice in the diamond suit.'

'That's what it's called!' exclaimed Elsie Bonneville. 'Restricted Choice, yes. It doesn't stand up to close examination, of course, because a 3-2 break is more likely.'

At the other table Brother Lucius and Brother Paulo faced Clarence and Lilian Prenderghast. Despite being in their late seventies, they had only recently taken up the game.

'This is our first big tournament,' said Clarence Prenderghast. 'I hope you won't mind if we make any silly mistakes.'

Brother Lucius smiled. 'Not at all,' he replied. 'You will find us most tolerant in that respect.'

The players drew their cards for this board:

```
North-South game          ♠ K Q J 10 4
Dealer South              ♡ 9 5 3
                          ◇ A
                          ♣ 8 6 5 4
         ♠ 7                              ♠ 8 6 5 3
         ♡ Q J 10 7 4      N              ♡ K 8 6
         ◇ 9 8 6        W     E           ◇ J 10 7 5 4 2
         ♣ Q 10 9 7       S               ♣ —
                          ♠ A 9 2
                          ♡ A 2
                          ◇ K Q 3
                          ♣ A K J 3 2
```

WEST	NORTH	EAST	SOUTH
Clarence	*Brother*	*Lilian*	*Brother*
Prenderghast	*Paulo*	*Prenderghast*	*Lucius*
–	–	–	2NT
Pass	3♡	Pass	3♠
Pass	3NT	Pass	4♣
Pass	4◇	Pass	6♠
Pass	Pass	Dble	All Pass

Brother Lucius cue-bid 4♣ on the way to the spade game, indicating that he had a maximum hand in support of spades. When the two monks reached a small slam, Lilian Prenderghast looked pointedly in her husband's direction and reached for the red Double card.

Clarence Prenderghast led the ♡Q and Lucius won with the ace. What on earth had prompted East's double? The trump suit was solid, so she must have intended her double as Lightner. In that case she was surely void in clubs. What could be done? He would have to strip the West hand and end-play him in clubs.

Lucius played a diamond to the ace and drew two rounds of trumps with the king and ace, West showing out on the second round. Two more rounds of diamonds stood up and Lucius threw the two heart losers from dummy. When he reverted to the trump suit this end position arose, with the lead in dummy:

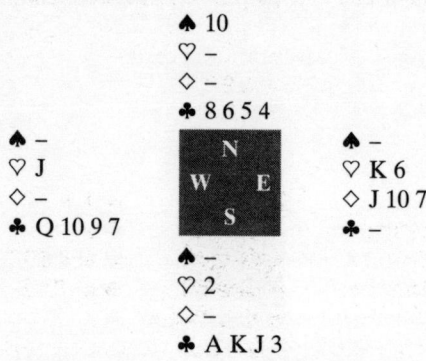

```
                    ♠ 10
                    ♡ –
                    ◇ –
                    ♣ 8 6 5 4
 ♠ –                            ♠ –
 ♡ J            N               ♡ K 6
 ◇ –         W     E            ◇ J 10 7
 ♣ Q 10 9 7     S               ♣ –
                    ♠ –
                    ♡ 2
                    ◇ –
                    ♣ A K J 3
```

Playing the last trump at this stage would not be good enough. West would discard a club and the defenders would score a heart and a club. 'Play a club,' said Brother Lucius.

He won the trick with the ace and led his last heart, ruffing in the dummy. West's last three cards were the Q-10-9 of clubs. When Lucius ducked a round of clubs Clarence Prenderghast had to win and lead into declarer's king-jack tenace. The slam had been made.

'You should have led a club at Trick 1, Clarence,' said Mrs Prenderghast. 'Surely you remember what Pam Johnson told us in last week's class. A double of a slam asks for a ruff.'

'I remembered that all right,' her husband replied. 'I thought you might be able to ruff a heart.'

'Don't be silly,' said Mrs Prenderghast. 'I had king-to-three in hearts. I can only ruff clubs. That's what you should have led.'

Clarence Prenderghast scratched his head, looking down at his scorecard. 'What does that come to?' he asked.

His wife consulted the scoring table. 'It's 1430 to them,' she replied. 'Lead a club and it would be a nice plus score to us.'

Brother Lucius leaned forward. 'It's 1690,' he said. 'Don't forget the double.'

Mrs Prenderghast looked up in some alarm. 'No, no, it wasn't a penalty double,' she said. 'It was one of those special doubles, asking for a club ruff. That doesn't affect the score, does it?'

Lucius smiled. 'I think you'll find that it does,' he said. 'Would you like me to call a director so we can check?'

'Well, I certainly wouldn't have doubled if I thought you'd get 1690,' declared Mrs Prenderghast. 'Pam Johnson never mentioned anything about that and she charges ten pounds a lesson.'

Back on the other table the players were about to bid the last board of the match.

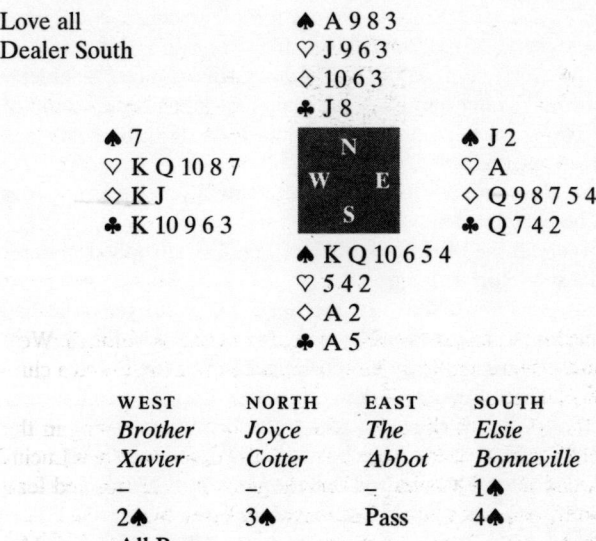

Love all
Dealer South

```
                    ♠ A 9 8 3
                    ♡ J 9 6 3
                    ◇ 10 6 3
                    ♣ J 8
  ♠ 7                              ♠ J 2
  ♡ K Q 10 8 7          N          ♡ A
  ◇ K J              W     E       ◇ Q 9 8 7 5 4
  ♣ K 10 9 6 3          S          ♣ Q 7 4 2
                    ♠ K Q 10 6 5 4
                    ♡ 5 4 2
                    ◇ A 2
                    ♣ A 5
```

WEST	NORTH	EAST	SOUTH
Brother	*Joyce*	*The*	*Elsie*
Xavier	*Cotter*	*Abbot*	*Bonneville*
–	–	–	1♠
2♠	3♠	Pass	4♠
All Pass			

Brother Xavier, whose Michaels cue bid had promised hearts and a minor, led the king of hearts against the spade game. Joyce Cotter adjusted her neck brace and laid out the dummy in four neat columns.

'Not much there for me, Joyce,' observed Elsie Bonneville, viewing the ace and two jacks with disfavour.

'I only showed a raise to Two Spades, dear,' her partner replied. 'With a sound raise I would bid Three Hearts instead.'

'On four to the jack?' exclaimed Elsie Bonneville. 'Hardly worth it when you have four-card support for my suit. We're much too high, anyway. There are five unavoidable losers.'

The Abbot overtook the king of hearts lead with the bare ace and switched to a low diamond, drawing the ace from declarer. Elsie Bonneville drew trumps in two rounds and then led a heart towards the dummy. Realising that it would expose the position if he rose with the queen, Brother Xavier played low.

'A king lead promises the queen, does it?' asked Elsie Bonneville.

The Abbot nodded encouragingly. 'That's right,' he said. Come on, you old dear. Put on the jack and go down gracefully.

Elsie Bonneville peered suspiciously at the Abbot. 'How many hearts did the Michaels bid show?' she said.

The Abbot did not like to be too helpful in such situations. Not that he would actually be unethical about it. 'It tends to vary according to the vulnerability,' he replied.

Elsie Bonneville considered the matter for a few more seconds, as if weighing up some 50:50 guess. 'Try the nine,' she said eventually.

Fearing the worst, the Abbot discarded a diamond. The elderly declarer returned to her hand with a trump and led another round of hearts. She could not be deprived of a club discard on the heart jack and the game was made.

The Abbot glared across the table. 'Lead anything else and it goes *two* down!' he exclaimed.

'A heart seemed the obvious lead,' Brother Xavier replied. 'I don't like to lead a singleton trump.'

The Abbot gave a sad shake of the head. Over the years, he had become accustomed to Brother Xavier blowing a trick with his opening leads. But two tricks? That was pushing things, even for him.

'Your bid of Three Spades worked out better than expected, Joyce,' said Elsie Bonneville. 'It gave us a nice top.'

Joyce Cotter looked excitedly at her partner. 'Yes, it was a bit bold,' she replied. 'I wouldn't have dared risk it on one of the higher tables!'

15.   Brother Xavier's Poor Session

The Abbot had rarely enjoyed an event less. Six rounds of green-point Swiss, played in an airless Winchester Sports Centre, and with only one round to go his team was lingering on Table 15.

The monastery team's final match was against the Upshot-Bagley family. The Abbot surveyed the two very tall sons, who would be the opponents at his table. No doubt they had picked up the rudiments of the game at some second-rate university. If they thought this entitled them to compete effectively against a Grandmaster with forty years of experience in the game . . . they would soon find out to the contrary.

This was the first board of the match:

```
Game all              ♠ Q 7
Dealer South          ♡ 10 9 7 4 2
                      ◇ A 5 3
                      ♣ 8 4 3
         ♠ 5 4 2          N          ♠ 8 3
         ♡ K Q J 3                   ♡ A 8 6 5
         ◇ J 4       W       E       ◇ Q 10 9 7 2
         ♣ J 9 7 2       S           ♣ 10 6
                      ♠ A K J 10 9 6
                      ♡ –
                      ◇ K 8 6
                      ♣ A K Q 5
```

WEST	NORTH	EAST	SOUTH
The	*Julian*	*Brother*	*Simon*
Abbot	*U-Bagley*	*Xavier*	*U-Bagley*
–	–	–	2♣
Pass	2◇	Pass	2♠
Pass	3♠	Pass	4♣
Pass	4◇	Pass	4♡
Pass	4♠	Pass	5♣
Pass	5♠	Pass	6♣
Pass	6♠	All Pass	

The Abbot, who had shown increasing signs of impatience as the auction dragged ever onwards, lost no time in placing the king of hearts on the table.

The tall declarer, who was wearing a Southampton away-kit football shirt, nodded happily as the dummy went down. 'Yes, we bid it well, Julian,' he said. 'You saw the point of my six-club bid? I was hoping you could show me third-round diamond control.'

'Yes, yes,' his partner replied.

'You'd already denied second-round diamond control by bidding Five Spades over Five Clubs, so . . .'

This was too much for the Abbot. 'It's customary to hold the post-mortem *after* the hand,' he informed his young opponent. 'You to play from the dummy, if it's not too much trouble.'

'Play low,' said Simon Upshot-Bagley. It was absolutely true, what his father had told them about the Abbot. Incredibly rude! How could they ever improve their game if they weren't allowed to discuss an interesting bidding situation when it came up?

Declarer ruffed the heart lead and saw that he would have to make arrangements for his fourth club in order to score twelve tricks. Without drawing any trumps, he played the ace and king of clubs. The ♣10 from East sounded a warning note and he crossed to the ace of diamonds to lead the third round of clubs towards his hand.

After a few seconds thought, Brother Xavier decided to ruff. His heart return was ruffed by the declarer, who proceeded to sit back in his chair, planning the remainder of the play. How could he avoid a diamond loser? It seemed that the only chance was to play one round of trumps, followed by the club queen. If East had started with a doubleton trump, he would not be able to ruff. A diamond could be thrown from dummy and it would then be possible to ruff a diamond.

Simon Upshot-Bagley drew one round of trumps with the ace and placed the queen of clubs on the table, throwing a diamond from dummy. Brother Xavier also discarded a diamond and declarer proceeded to cash the diamond king and ruff a diamond in dummy. He returned to his hand with yet another heart ruff and drew the outstanding trumps. The slam was his.

'It's no better if I don't ruff the third club,' observed Brother Xavier. 'He wins with the queen and ruffs the fourth club high.'

'Obviously,' grunted the Abbot. 'If we could have defeated it, we would have done.'

Simon Upshot-Bagley turned towards the Abbot. 'I think a diamond lead beats it,' he said. 'If I win with the king and use the diamond ace as an entry to lead the third round of clubs towards my hand, East can ruff and cash a diamond.'

The Abbot had now heard everything. Not only was the young man wearing entirely unsuitable sporting apparel, he was also indulging in gratuitous criticism of his opponents' play. Lead a diamond from jack doubleton when he had a solid sequence in hearts? No-one outside a madhouse would consider it. 'You can cross to dummy with a trump instead of a diamond, can't you?'

Brother Xavier shook his head. 'That's no good. I duck the third round of clubs then, allowing the queen to win. If he ruffs the fourth round of clubs with the seven, I can overruff. If he plays loser-on-loser, throwing a diamond on the fourth club, you can remove dummy's last trump.'

At the other table Brother Lucius and Brother Paulo faced the boys' parents. Dennis Upshot-Bagley had recently retired after thirty years of teaching history at Winchester College. His wife, Phillippa, was a prominent fund raiser for the local Conservative organisation.

Love all
Dealer North

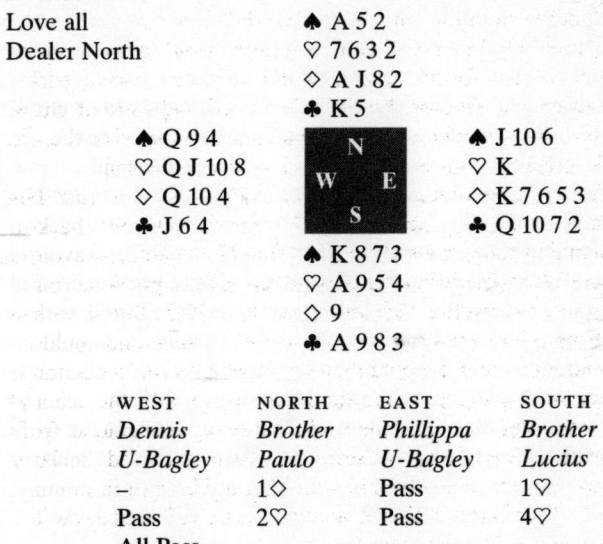

```
                    ♠ A 5 2
                    ♡ 7 6 3 2
                    ◇ A J 8 2
                    ♣ K 5
♠ Q 9 4                          ♠ J 10 6
♡ Q J 10 8          N           ♡ K
◇ Q 10 4          W   E          ◇ K 7 6 5 3
♣ J 6 4             S            ♣ Q 10 7 2
                    ♠ K 8 7 3
                    ♡ A 9 5 4
                    ◇ 9
                    ♣ A 9 8 3
```

WEST	NORTH	EAST	SOUTH
Dennis	Brother	Phillippa	Brother
U-Bagley	Paulo	U-Bagley	Lucius
–	1◇	Pass	1♡
Pass	2♡	Pass	4♡
All Pass			

Dennis Upshot-Bagley, whose receding hair was carefully arranged across his forehead, led the ♡Q against Brother Lucius's heart game. East played the king and, after a brief pause, Lucius allowed this card to win. A trump return would not have helped his cause but, as Lucius had suspected, East had no further trump to play. The jack of spades return was won in the dummy and Lucius cashed his other spade winner before embarking on a crossruff.

The ace of diamonds and a diamond ruff were followed by the king and ace of clubs and a club ruff in dummy. A second diamond ruff in declarer's hand left these cards still to be played:

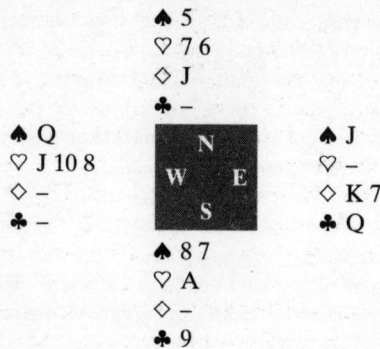

```
                    ♠ 5
                    ♡ 7 6
                    ◇ J
                    ♣ —
      ♠ Q                         ♠ J
      ♡ J 10 8        N           ♡ —
      ◇ —         W       E       ◇ K 7
      ♣ —             S           ♣ Q
                    ♠ 8 7
                    ♡ A
                    ◇ —
                    ♣ 9
```

When Lucius led his last club, Dennis Upshot-Bagley ruffed with the eight. 'Throw the spade,' instructed Brother Lucius.

Had declarer made the mistake of winning the first round of trumps, back at Trick 1, West would now have been able to kill the contract by drawing two further rounds of trumps. As it was, he could only return a trump to declarer's ace. A spade ruff in dummy then brought Brother Lucius's total to ten tricks.

Dennis Upshot-Bagley unscrewed the top from an ancient Osmiroid pen, one that had delivered many a damning verdict on fourth-form history essays. 'I nearly doubled, Phillippa,' he observed, as he wrote down the score. 'I had four good trumps and an honour in every suit.'

'Just as well you didn't,' his expensively-coiffed wife replied. 'I had an honour in every suit, too. It's surprising they were in game, really.'

The cards were running strongly in the North-South direction. Back on the other table, Simon Upshot-Bagley had just arrived in another slam:

North-South game
Dealer South

```
              ♠ 9 7 5 3
              ♡ K 4 2
              ◇ 8
              ♣ K Q J 10 6
♠ J 4                        ♠ K Q 10 8 6 2
♡ J 10 8 5      N            ♡ 6
◇ K Q J 10 5  W   E          ◇ 6 4
♣ 7 2           S            ♣ 9 8 4 3
              ♠ A
              ♡ A Q 9 7 3
              ◇ A 9 7 3 2
              ♣ A 5
```

WEST	NORTH	EAST	SOUTH
The	*Julian*	*Brother*	*Simon*
Abbot	*U-Bagley*	*Xavier*	*U-Bagley*
–	–	–	1♡
Pass	2♣	Pass	2◇
Pass	3♡	Pass	6♡
All Pass			

With a martyred air, the Abbot thumbed through his cards. This time his honour sequence was four-deep. He had strong trumps, too. Surely it was absolutely clear-cut to lead the king of diamonds. If it turned out that jack doubleton in the unbid suit was a winner, and the young declarer prattled on about it in his usual fashion, he would seriously consider giving up the game. The Abbot placed the diamond king on the table and down went the dummy.

'I didn't like to respond One Spade on four small cards,' said Julian Upshot-Bagley. 'A lot of players do, I realise. You know Steve Newbury. He says he *always* bids a four-card major, even it's only five-high!'

His brother liked the look of what he saw in the dummy. 'You bid it excellently, Julian,' he replied. 'The response in clubs was much more helpful.'

With some difficulty the Abbot refrained from making any comment. The opponents were inexperienced, yes, but surely someone should have told them what poor manners it was to praise their own bidding instead of proceeding with the play.

'If you respond One Spade instead, I don't think we'd have bid the slam,' continued the South player.

'Are you claiming the contract?' demanded the Abbot. 'If not, perhaps we'd better play the hand.'

Simon Upshot-Bagley turned towards the Abbot. 'I hope you don't mind me saying this,' he observed, 'but your attitude is rather spoiling our enjoyment of the event. There's not much point in playing if all you want to do is rush through the hands and get back home as soon as possible.'

The Abbot blinked. Rush through the hands? He must be joking. It was his own endless post-mortems, both before the play and afterwards, that were spoiling everyone's enjoyment.

The young declarer won the diamond lead and paused to consider the play. If trumps were 3-2, there would be an easy thirteen tricks. What if trumps were 4-1? It would be inconvenient to lose a trump trick later, when the diamonds were exposed and dummy's trumps had gone. It seemed that it would be better to surrender a trump trick now, while dummy still had some trumps to deal with a diamond continuation.

At Trick 2 Simon Upshot-Bagley led the three of trumps, the five appearing on his left. His equally tall brother reached for dummy's king but declarer shook his head. 'No, play low,' he said.

Brother Xavier won with the six but had no constructive return. When he eventually played the ♠K, declarer won with the ace and ruffed a diamond. After cashing the bare king of trumps, he returned to hand with the ♣A. He then drew the outstanding trumps, delighted to find that they were indeed 4-1 and that his safety play had been productive. 'The rest are mine,' he said, facing his cards with a flourish.

The Abbot exhaled deeply as he returned his cards to the wallet. What right did opponents have to play so well on Table 15 of a local Swiss? If declarer hadn't ducked that trump, he would have gone down.

The Abbot peered at his tall opponent. 'I suppose you'll be telling me now that a spade lead from jack-one would have worked better.'

Simon Upshot-Bagley looked back uncertainly. 'A spade lead is no good,' he replied. 'I had a singleton ace of spades.'

The Abbot was determined to point out that the youngster's own table manners had been far from satisfactory. 'I was recalling that earlier deal,' he persisted. 'The spade slam where you said that I should have led a diamond.'

Brother Xavier leaned forward. 'I think we needed a club lead on this one, Abbot,' he said. 'If declarer ducks a trump then, you can lead another club, killing the dummy.'

Pretending not to hear, the Abbot peered across at the other table of their match. 'Ah, they've finished,' he said, rising to his feet.

This was definitely the last time he supported one of these local events, thought the Abbot, as he made his way towards Lucius and

Paulo. Unbelievably low standard. It was a complete waste of his time playing with partners and opponents who didn't even recognise the soundness of leading from a K-Q-J sequence.

'We're quite good,' said Brother Lucius, as the Abbot took his seat. 'At least we should end with a big win.'

'I wouldn't bank on it,' declared the Abbot. 'Xavier's had a bit of a nightmare at our table. Still, here he comes. Don't say anything.'

16.   No Justice at St Titus

The seventh round of the Thursday Pairs brought Lucius and Paulo to the Abbot's table.

'Ah, the world's two worst overbidders have arrived,' observed the Abbot. 'Good news, partner. We won't have to defend tightly to get this particular pair down.'

Brother Paulo smiled as he took his seat. 'I cannot remember the last time I overbid,' he replied. 'I may take the occasional favourable view of a hand but that's not what I call overbidding.'

This was the first board of the round:

Game all
Dealer South

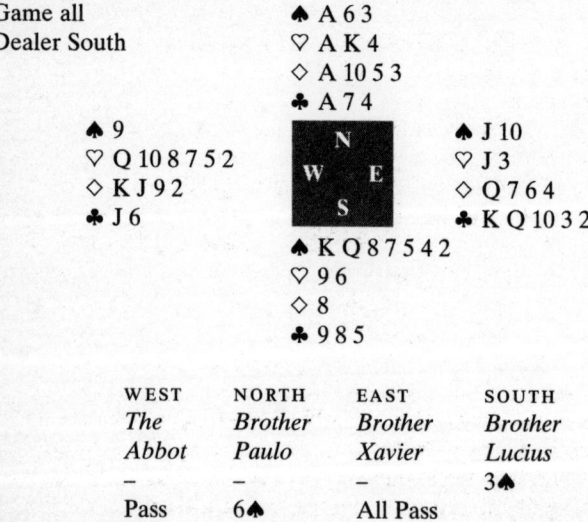

```
                    ♠ A 6 3
                    ♡ A K 4
                    ◇ A 10 5 3
                    ♣ A 7 4
  ♠ 9                              ♠ J 10
  ♡ Q 10 8 7 5 2      N            ♡ J 3
  ◇ K J 9 2        W     E         ◇ Q 7 6 4
  ♣ J 6               S            ♣ K Q 10 3 2
                    ♠ K Q 8 7 5 4 2
                    ♡ 9 6
                    ◇ 8
                    ♣ 9 8 5
```

WEST	NORTH	EAST	SOUTH
The	*Brother*	*Brother*	*Brother*
Abbot	*Paulo*	*Xavier*	*Lucius*
–	–	–	3♠
Pass	6♠	All Pass	

The Abbot led the two of diamonds and down went the dummy.

'You will hardly say I have overbid this hand!' exclaimed Brother Paulo, looking fondly at his four aces.

No indeed, thought the Abbot. Why, if declarer held the proverbial K-Q-J-x-x-x and three doubletons, the contract would be only one down.

Brother Lucius surveyed the dummy with his usual impassive expression. He would need a squeeze of some sort but prospects were very poor. Perhaps he should play low from dummy on the first trick. If East had to expend his guard on dummy's ◇10 a squeeze on West might be possible. 'Small, please,' said Brother Lucius.

East won the first trick with the queen of diamonds and the Abbot was now in sole control of both red suits. Brother Lucius won the king of clubs return with dummy's ace and drew trumps with the king and ace. He then cashed the diamond ace and ruffed a diamond, just in case this would remove a diamond guard from East. The run of declarer's spades led to this end position:

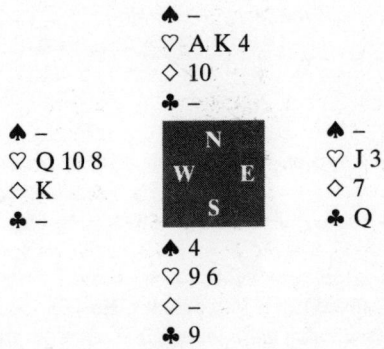

```
              ♠ —
              ♡ A K 4
              ◇ 10
              ♣ —
  ♠ —                      ♠ —
  ♡ Q 10 8    N            ♡ J 3
  ◇ K       W   E          ◇ 7
  ♣ —         S            ♣ Q
              ♠ 4
              ♡ 9 6
              ◇ —
              ♣ 9
```

When the last spade was led the Abbot had to abandon one of the red suits and the slam was made.

Brother Paulo was much amused. 'No need to defend carefully, as you say, Abbot,' he declared. 'Only the two of diamonds lead forces Brother Xavier to surrender his precious queen. Lead any of the other twelve cards in your hand and you beat the slam easily!'

The Abbot surveyed Brother Paulo in disbelief. 'If I ever find myself laughing at someone else's misfortune, I will resign my stewardship,' he declared. 'Any top-class player would lead the two of diamonds from my hand.'

The Abbot was hoping for better luck as he picked up his cards for the second board.

North-South game   ♠ J 7 5
Dealer East   ♡ A 4
                          ◇ K Q 4 3
                          ♣ Q J 9 5

	♠ Q 10 9 2		♠ 3
	♡ J 5 2	N	♡ K Q 10 8 7 3
	◇ 10 8 2	W E	◇ 9 7 6
	♣ K 8 7	S	♣ 6 3 2

                        ♠ A K 8 6 4
                        ♡ 9 6
                        ◇ A J 5
                        ♣ A 10 4

WEST	NORTH	EAST	SOUTH
The	*Brother*	*Brother*	*Brother*
Abbot	*Paulo*	*Xavier*	*Lucius*
–	–	2♡	2♠
Pass	3♡	Pass	4♠
All Pass			

The Abbot led the two of hearts, in response to his partner's weak-
two bid. Brother Lucius won with dummy's ace and played a trump to
the ace. On this trick the Abbot dropped a smooth ten.

Lucius had intended to lead low towards the jack on the second
round of trumps, a safety play against a 4-1 break. The appearance of
the ten on his left caused him to reconsider. East was unlikely to hold
four spades after his Weak Two opening. The most likely position was
surely that the Abbot held Q-10 doubleton. Playing for this chance,
Brother Lucius continued with king of trumps.

With the air of Belladonna in his prime, the Abbot contributed the
two of trumps to the trick. He turned to observe Brother Lucius's
reaction as East showed out but he was as impassive as ever. Still,
thought the Abbot, it wouldn't save him from a bad result on the
board.

Brother Lucius now moved to the diamond suit. When West
followed three times he was able to discard his heart loser on the
fourth round. The Abbot ruffed, cashed the queen of trumps, then
forced declarer with a heart.

'Unfortunately, I cannot take the club finesse now,' said Brother
Lucius. 'Excellent defence, Abbot, I will have to play clubs from hand.
Just the ten.'

'It doesn't cost you, as it happens,' replied the Abbot. 'I have the king over here.'

Brother Paulo opened the scoresheet. 'Everyone has made 620,' he announced. 'If you lead low to the jack on the second round of trumps, you lose one trump, one heart and a club.'

The Abbot sat back in his chair, waiting for the change of round to be called. Absolutely typical! His brightest defensive effort for ages had gained not a single match-point. That was the problem with bridge as a game. The final ranking list rarely reflected the skill of the players involved.

The Abbot was hoping for some respite on the next round, but it was his least favourite opponents, Brother Cameron and Brother Damien, who arrived at the table.

'Unbelievable that I should make that one,' declared Brother Cameron, sinking into the South seat. 'What on earth was the point of him holding on to the king of clubs? I'd already shown out of the suit.'

'Are my ears failing me, Xavier?' asked the Abbot. 'I didn't hear this pair greet their opponents.'

'Evening, Abbot,' said Brother Cameron. 'You wouldn't believe the poor standard of defence we've had against us tonight.'

'Did you enter these portals solely to criticise your fellow Brothers?' demanded the Abbot. 'It's one of the world's greatest mysteries why I ever agreed to admit you.'

It was well known that Brother Cameron's father had eased the wheels by making a substantial contribution to the new St Titus manuscript library. The Abbot had thought several times since that he would rather do without both the library and Brother Cameron.

Brother Cameron picked up this hand:

> ♠ A K Q
> ♡ 8 7 3
> ◇ Q 3
> ♣ A J 8 5 2

Vulnerable against not, he opened One Club. Brother Damien responded One Diamond and Brother Xavier entered with One Heart. What now? There was little merit in Two Clubs, on such a modest suit. Nor was 1NT without a heart stop attractive. 'One Spade,' said Brother Cameron.

His partner raised to Four Spades and this was the full deal:

North-South game
Dealer South

```
              ♠ 7 5 4 2
              ♡ J 5
              ◇ A K J 10 6 4
              ♣ 6
♠ 10 8 6 3              ♠ J 9
♡ Q 10 4       N       ♡ A K 9 6 2
◇ 8 7 2    W     E     ◇ 9 5
♣ Q 9 3        S       ♣ K 10 7 4
              ♠ A K Q
              ♡ 8 7 3
              ◇ Q 3
              ♣ A J 8 5 2
```

WEST	NORTH	EAST	SOUTH
The	*Brother*	*Brother*	*Brother*
Abbot	*Damien*	*Xavier*	*Cameron*
–	–	–	1♣
Pass	1◇	1♡	1♠
Pass	4♠	All Pass	

The Abbot led a heart against the spade game and the defenders played three rounds of the suit, forcing the dummy to ruff. All would be easy if the outstanding trumps were 3-3 but Brother Cameron could see a fair chance even if West held four trumps. He crossed to his ace of clubs and ruffed a club. A trump to the ace permitted a second club ruff, both defenders following. Two more rounds of trumps left West with the only trump outstanding. Brother Cameron then turned to the diamond suit, needing the Abbot to follow to three rounds. When this came to pass, declarer ended with six trump tricks and four side-suit winners. Game made.

'You only had three spades?' grunted the Abbot. 'Did you mis-sort your hand?'

'Seemed the right bid,' Brother Cameron replied. 'Don't know what else I could have said.'

The Abbot raised his eyes to the ceiling. It was typical of his luck that Brother Cameron should make some absurd call and find that it paid off.

'Would you like to see the scoresheet, Abbot?' asked Brother Damien.

The Abbot pretended not to hear. Minus 620 would not exactly exert the scorer. Perhaps luck would turn in his direction on the next deal.

Game all   ♠ 8 7 4 3
Dealer East   ♡ 6 5 3
                 ◇ A 7 2
                 ♣ K Q 5

♠ K Q J 6 5   ♠ A 10 9 2
♡ 9 7   ♡ 10 8 2
◇ K 8   N   ◇ J 10 6 4
♣ 8 4 3 2   W   E   ♣ J 6
            S

                 ♠ –
                 ♡ A K Q J 4
                 ◇ Q 9 5 3
                 ♣ A 10 9 7

WEST	NORTH	EAST	SOUTH
The	*Brother*	*Brother*	*Brother*
Abbot	*Damien*	*Xavier*	*Cameron*
–	–	Pass	1♡
1♠	2♡	2♠	3♠
Pass	5♡	Pass	6♡
All Pass			

An adventurous auction carried the novice pair to a small slam and the Abbot led the king of spades.

'You bid Five Hearts on that?' gasped the Abbot, as the dummy appeared.

'I must be filling his minors in,' Brother Damien replied. 'I intended the Five Heart bid to ask for good trumps.'

Brother Cameron paused to plan the play. The Abbot was not one to overcall on minimal values and was likely to hold the ◇K. All would be well, in diamonds at least, if West held ◇K-J or ◇K-10 doubleton. After dropping the king in two rounds, a finesse of the nine would bring in the suit. If instead West held K-8, K-6 or K-4, it might be possible to ruff the fourth round of diamonds in dummy.

Brother Cameron ruffed the spade lead and led a diamond, ducking in dummy when the eight appeared from West. With nothing better to do, the Abbot played another spade. Brother Cameron ruffed again, drew two rounds of trumps, and then played a second diamond. With a shake of the head, the Abbot tossed the ◇K on to the table. Dummy's ace won the trick and a third round of diamonds was taken by South's queen, West discarding a spade. Declarer ruffed the fourth round of diamonds to leave these cards outstanding:

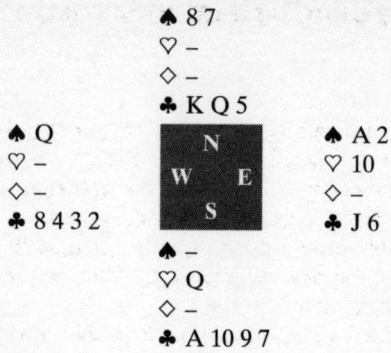

```
            ♠ 8 7
            ♡ –
            ◇ –
            ♣ K Q 5
♠ Q                          ♠ A 2
♡ –          N              ♡ 10
◇ –       W     E           ◇ –
♣ 8 4 3 2    S              ♣ J 6
            ♠ –
            ♡ Q
            ◇ –
            ♣ A 10 9 7
```

Brother Cameron called for the king of clubs. When he continued with the queen of clubs, the jack appeared from East. 'They're all there now,' he said. 'I overtake with the ace and draw the last trump.'

The Abbot closed his eyes, as if in pain. 'A very reasonable contract,' he observed. 'You only needed me to hold king doubleton in diamonds, along with precisely two trumps, and the jack of clubs to come down.'

'I'm not sure your list of conditions is complete, Abbot,' said Brother Xavier. 'Young Brother Cameron had to play it quite well, too.'

'The hand played itself,' muttered the Abbot. So far as he could see, there had been no merit whatsoever in the two tops that had placed themselves on the youngsters' scorecards. It only served to support the theory he had been mulling over earlier. Bridge was hardly a game of skill at all, nowadays.

'Would you like to see the scoresheet?' asked Brother Damien, somewhat louder than on the previous board.

'I'll deprive myself of that pleasure,' replied the Abbot. 'I can't believe anyone else thought a 2% slam was worth bidding.'

17. The Abbot's Charitable Visit

Somewhat against his better judgement, the Abbot had agreed to give an instructive talk to the bridge section of the local Women's Institute. This was to be followed by a short duplicate session, in which he would partner Winifred Stoope, chairperson of the group.

'A very enjoyable presentation, Abbot,' declared Winifred Stoope, as they headed for the playing area. 'I'm afraid I disagreed with your analysis on one hand, though.'

The Abbot wiped the perspiration from his brow. Most of the audience were fairly elderly, doubtless with poor circulation, but was it really necessary for the hall to be so hot? 'Which hand was that?' he enquired.

'I think it was your third hand,' Winifred Stoope continued. 'You said that it would be wrong to draw trumps immediately because you needed to ruff two diamonds in dummy.'

'Yes, yes, that's right,' replied the Abbot.

'Well, that policy may happen to work on your particular hand,' said Mrs Stoope, 'but it's very poor advice in general. I've gone down many a time by failing to draw trumps.'

The Abbot surveyed his partner for the approaching session uncertainly. Was the old dear serious or making a somewhat feeble joke? 'I didn't intend it as general advice,' he replied. 'I was just explaining how that particular hand should be played.'

'I think you may have confused some of our members,' declared Mrs Stoope. 'Still, never mind, it was very good of you to give up your time.'

The session began and on the first round the Abbot and his partner faced two elderly ladies with tight, white-haired perms.

'You'll laugh when you hear our names, Abbot,' declared the taller of the two.

'Yes, we're Daisy and Maisie,' said the other. 'Everyone has a good laugh at that. You know, because our names rhyme.'

With a Herculean effort the Abbot managed a polite smile. Yes, the evening had been a bundle of fun so far. What with rhyming names as well, one could almost die laughing. Now, what awaited him on this deal?

124

Game all
Dealer West

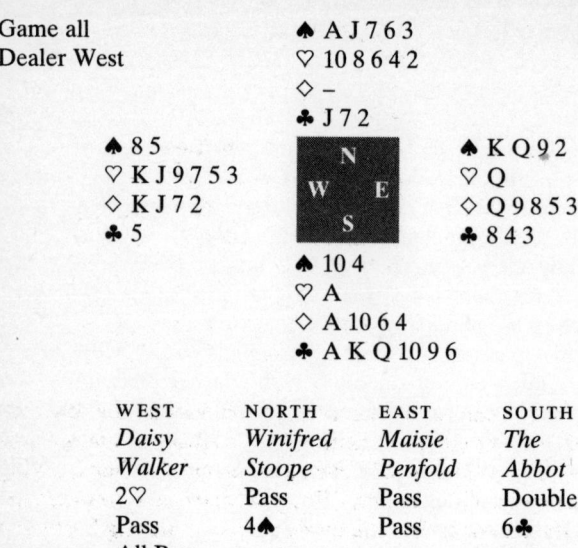

```
                        ♠ A J 7 6 3
                        ♡ 10 8 6 4 2
                        ◇ –
                        ♣ J 7 2
        ♠ 8 5                              ♠ K Q 9 2
        ♡ K J 9 7 5 3                      ♡ Q
        ◇ K J 7 2                          ◇ Q 9 8 5 3
        ♣ 5                                ♣ 8 4 3
                        ♠ 10 4
                        ♡ A
                        ◇ A 10 6 4
                        ♣ A K Q 10 9 6
```

WEST	NORTH	EAST	SOUTH
Daisy	*Winifred*	*Maisie*	*The*
Walker	*Stoope*	*Penfold*	*Abbot*
2♡	Pass	Pass	Double
Pass	4♠	Pass	6♣
All Pass			

The five of trumps was led and Winifred Stoope laid out the dummy.
The Abbot surveyed it as if it were some unreasonable tax demand.
Where in Heaven's name had she found that response of Four Spades?
Two Spades would have been plenty, facing a protective double.

Winifred Stoope smiled across the table. 'Ron Klinger says you
should bid up when you have five-card support for partner,' she said.
'You didn't bid spades, I realise, but a double of one major promises
the other. I was explaining that to my husband only the other night.'

Maisie Penfold looked down at her own hand. It was a pity that
Winnie hadn't put the Abbot back to spades. She'd have had a nice
double of that contract.

The Abbot turned his mind to the play. What was this trump lead?
After any other lead he could have ruffed three diamonds in the
dummy. He won the trump lead in his hand and ruffed a diamond. A
heart to the ace was followed by a second diamond ruff. He then
crossed to his hand with a heart ruff, East throwing a diamond. Three
more rounds of trumps left these cards still to be played:

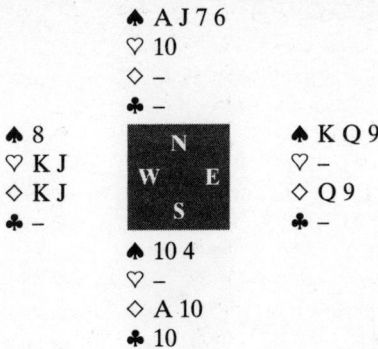

```
            ♠ A J 7 6
            ♡ 10
            ◇ –
            ♣ –
 ♠ 8                      ♠ K Q 9
 ♡ K J        N          ♡ –
 ◇ K J     W     E       ◇ Q 9
 ♣ –          S          ♣ –
            ♠ 10 4
            ♡ –
            ◇ A 10
            ♣ 10
```

When the Abbot played his last trump, West and the dummy both discarded hearts. Maisie Penfold, sitting East, had no card to spare. If she threw a spade, declarer would duck a spade into her hand, setting up three spade tricks in the dummy. When she chose to throw the nine of diamonds the Abbot cashed the diamond ace, removing East's last card in the suit. He then ran the ten of spades to the queen.

Maisie Penfold gazed at her last two cards, the ♠K-9, then surveyed the ♠A-J awaiting them in the dummy. 'That's very unlucky,' she declared.

'You have to lead a spade?' said the Abbot exultantly.

'Yes,' replied Maisie Penfold. 'Sorry, partner. I should have kept another diamond.'

'You should have done,' Daisy Walker replied. 'Still, never mind, dear. Most people would have done the same.'

The Abbot looked in turn at the three ladies around him. Surely his great play hadn't gone completely unappreciated? 'It makes no difference if you keep another diamond,' he said. 'I can set up . . .'

'It's very gallant of you to come to my rescue,' said Maisie Penfold, patting the Abbot on the hand, 'but I'm quite prepared to take the blame when I make a mistake.' She gave a rueful smile. 'It happens often enough.'

A round or two later the Abbot faced two smartly dressed women in their fifties.

'Betty, here, is our best player,' announced Mrs Stoope. 'She plays for the county!'

The Abbot, who was well acquainted with the county's top players, cast an eye over the purple-clad occupant of the South seat. Plays for the county? He had never seen the woman before! Presumably she had played in some social inter-county event, two decades ago, and had been dining out on the achievement ever since. 'I'm pleased to meet you,' he said.

Betty Tivendale had a chance to display her skills on this board:

North-South game
Dealer South

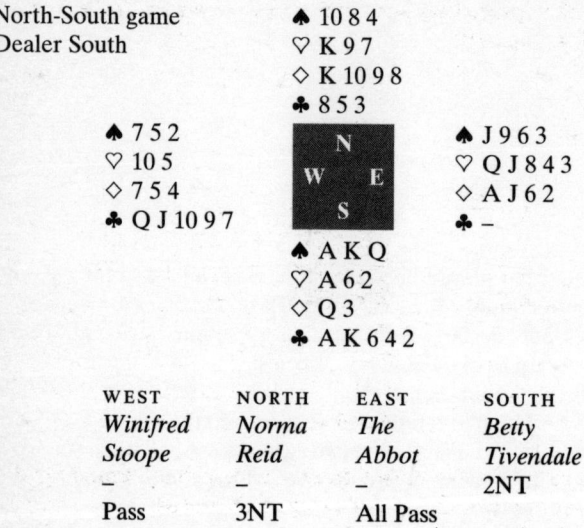

```
                    ♠ 10 8 4
                    ♡ K 9 7
                    ◇ K 10 9 8
                    ♣ 8 5 3
    ♠ 7 5 2                          ♠ J 9 6 3
    ♡ 10 5              N            ♡ Q J 8 4 3
    ◇ 7 5 4         W     E          ◇ A J 6 2
    ♣ Q J 10 9 7       S            ♣ —
                    ♠ A K Q
                    ♡ A 6 2
                    ◇ Q 3
                    ♣ A K 6 4 2
```

WEST	NORTH	EAST	SOUTH
Winifred	*Norma*	*The*	*Betty*
Stoope	*Reid*	*Abbot*	*Tivendale*
–	–	–	2NT
Pass	3NT	All Pass	

Winifred Stoope led the queen of clubs and down went the dummy. 'It's a minimum of 26 points between the hands, partner,' observed Norma Reid, in a Scottish accent. 'We had to be in game.'

'Well bid, dear,' replied Betty Tivendale.

The Abbot gritted his teeth. How many boards were there going to be? He would make up some excuse if they ever invited him to come again. Or perhaps he could send Brother Xavier instead. Yes, see how he enjoyed it.

The Abbot discarded a heart on the club lead and Betty Tivendale won with the ace. Moving an index finger backwards and forwards, she proceeded to count the top tricks in her own hand and the dummy. By the Abbot's reckoning of her finger movements, she had seven tricks on top.

At Trick 2 Betty Tivendale led the queen of diamonds from her hand. Hoping to cut declarer off from the dummy, the Abbot allowed this card to win. The elegantly coiffed declarer, who rarely encountered defensive hold-ups at this particular venue, paused to consider her next move. Should she finesse the ten of diamonds? The finesse was surely likely to fail after East had turned up with no clubs to his partner's five. Perhaps a throw-in would work instead?

Yes, East's heart discard had surely been from his longest suit, which must be of at least five cards. In that case West could hold no more than a doubleton heart.

Betty Tivendale cashed the king of clubs, drawing a diamond discard from East, then played off her remaining five winners in the majors. These cards remained:

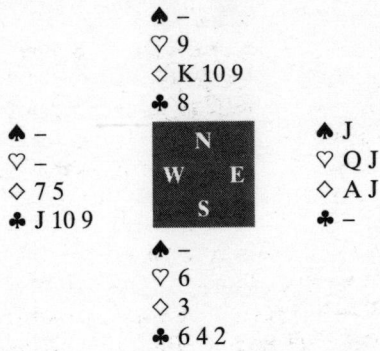

```
              ♠ —
              ♡ 9
              ◇ K 10 9
              ♣ 8
  ♠ —                        ♠ J
  ♡ —          N             ♡ Q J
  ◇ 7 5      W   E           ◇ A J
  ♣ J 10 9     S             ♣ —
              ♠ —
              ♡ 6
              ◇ 3
              ♣ 6 4 2
```

A heart exit threw the Abbot on lead and, at the finish, he had to surrender a ninth trick to dummy's king of diamonds.

'Exquisitely played, Betty,' declared the Scotswoman sitting North. 'Don't you think so, Abbot? If only we could all play so well.'

The Abbot restrained himself from passing comment. Declarer had completely butchered the diamond suit, then brought off a lucky recovery – that's what had happened. Had she played a low diamond to the ten on the first round, he would have had no counter. If he allowed the ten to win, declarer would simply clear a second diamond trick. If instead he won with the jack, she would be able to overtake the queen on the second round.

'Would you have played it the same way, Abbot?' Winifred Stoope enquired.

The Abbot shook his head. 'No, I would have . . .'

'Neither would I,' continued Winifred Stoope. She looked admiringly at the South player. 'I suppose that's why Betty plays for the county and we don't.'

The last round of the evening was played against Eileen Davey, who was confined to a wheelchair, and her younger sister, Joyce. Winifred Stoope played the first hand somewhat carelessly, scoring a bottom in 1NT. The Abbot then arrived in a slam.

Love all
Dealer South

	♠ K Q 7	
	♡ Q J 9	
	◇ A 9 7	
	♣ 10 8 3 2	

♠ 4 2		♠ 9 5 3
♡ 5	N	♡ 10 8 7 6 2
◇ K J 8 6 5	W E	◇ 10 4 3
♣ K J 9 6 5	S	♣ Q 7

	♠ A J 10 8 6	
	♡ A K 4 3	
	◇ Q 2	
	♣ A 4	

WEST	NORTH	EAST	SOUTH
Eileen	*Winifred*	*Joyce*	*The*
Davey	*Stoope*	*Davey*	*Abbot*
–	–	–	1♠
2NT	4♠	Pass	6♠
All Pass			

Partnering a true bridge player, the Abbot would have cue-bid 5♣ at his second turn. In the present circumstances he decided that a direct jump to the slam was the best tactics. If West were to cash two diamond winners, he would have to make his apologies and head for the exit. At least the ordeal would be over.

Eileen Davey peered up from her wheelchair. 'My 2NT bid was the unusual no-trump,' she informed the Abbot.

'Yes, yes,' replied the Abbot. 'It's you to lead.'

'It doesn't show a strong hand,' Eileen Davey continued. 'It shows the two minor suits. Do you play that?'

'Everyone plays that,' declared the Abbot, whose patience was running low. 'It's your opening lead.'

Eileen Davey shared a glance with her sister. Very gruff tone of voice he had, for a priest. It was a pity Winifred couldn't have found a more personable speaker. The man who had addressed them on marsh wildflowers last week had been much more pleasant. When she'd told him all about her grandchildren afterwards, he'd been most interested. This Abbot character didn't look like he would be interested in anyone's grandchildren.

Winifred Stoope leaned forward in friendly fashion. 'Your lead, Eileen,' she said. 'It's getting rather late. The Abbot's talk went on longer than we expected.'

West led her singleton heart and the Abbot inspected the dummy in learned fashion. If he could duck a round of clubs to West, there would be a straightforward simple squeeze in the minors. If East won the conceded club trick she could – in theory – switch to a diamond, breaking up the squeeze. What other chances were there? Perhaps he could simply run his winners in the majors. The old dear on the left would doubtless keep a couple of king-ones, allowing an easy endplay.

'Don't think I'm hurrying you, Abbot,' said Winifred Stoope, 'but most of the other tables have finished play and we do have to be out of the hall by ten o'clock.'

The Abbot raised an eyebrow. It was acceptable to dither for ages over your opening lead, apparently. If anyone spent a moment or two planning the play of a difficult hand, this was out of order. He won the heart lead in the dummy, drew trumps in three rounds and then returned to dummy with the jack of hearts. 'Eight of clubs,' said the Abbot.

When the seven appeared from East, the Abbot's eyes lit up. Just what the doctor ordered! He followed with the four from his hand and West – the safe hand – had to win the trick. The squeeze was now guaranteed.

Eileen Davey thumbed through the remaining cards in her hand and eventually pulled out a low diamond. The Abbot ran this successfully to his queen and twelve tricks had been made.

'You're getting a bit tired, Eileen,' observed the East player. 'Play a club at the end and he goes down. I had the queen of clubs.'

'I was on a guess,' her partner replied. 'I hoped you would hold the queen of diamonds.'

Winifred Stoope rose to her feet. 'Don't forget to leave the hall tidy, everyone,' she called out.

The Abbot would normally have explained to all and sundry how he would have made the contract anyway, even on a club return. Explaining a simple squeeze to the present company was not to be contemplated, however. It would be a lifetime's work.

'We didn't do particularly well, Abbot,' declared Winifred Stoope, struggling into her overcoat. 'You were given a couple of slams but I don't think it will be enough to put us in the points.'

'There's a lot of luck involved over such a short session,' observed the Abbot.

'I usually do quite well with my regular partner,' Winifred Stoope declared. 'Still, never mind. I'm sure you tried your best.'

18.   Mrs Parrott's Clever Endplay

'I don't think I'll bother entering the Southampton League next year,' declared the Abbot, straining his eyes as he searched for a parking space. 'Playing in these minor competitions is no more than an act of charity. It gives the local teams a chance to practise against strong opposition but we get nothing out of it ourselves.'

'Can you squeeze in behind that Rover?' suggested Brother Xavier.

'Much too tight,' replied the Abbot. 'I don't want to put my paintwork at risk.'

An amused Brother Paulo nudged Brother Lucius. The Abbot's car was worth £300 at the very most. An extra scratch or two would hardly be noticed.

The Abbot found a parking spot some hundred yards beyond the home of Cedric Parrott, the opponents' captain, and the four monks shielded their heads from the rain as they walked back along the lamp-lit street.

'If we set our minds to it, we could win this league every year,' declared the Abbot. 'It's difficult to play at your best in such a meaningless competition. That's the problem.'

The four monks were welcomed into the detached house and the match was soon under way. The Abbot was facing two middle-aged men, unknown to him, when a remarkable auction occurred.

Game all
Dealer North

	♠ Q 9 6 2	
	♡ A K 8 2	
	◇ J 6	
	♣ Q 4 2	
♠ 7 5 3	**N**	♠ A K J 10 8 4
♡ Q 6	**W E**	♡ J 9 5
◇ 10 8 3	**S**	◇ 7
♣ 10 9 8 5 3		♣ J 7 6
	♠ –	
	♡ 10 7 4 3	
	◇ A K Q 9 5 4 2	
	♣ A K	

WEST	NORTH	EAST	SOUTH
The	*Dr*	*Brother*	*Dr*
Abbot	*Moore*	*Xavier*	*Gorse*
–	1NT	2♠	7♦
All Pass			

The Abbot led a low trump and down went the dummy. Dr Gorse, whose green pullover had seen many years service, surveyed the dummy anxiously. He was one trick short. What could be done?

If either defender held ♡Q-J doubleton he would be OK, of course. If East held a singleton ♡9, this could be pinned by a lead of the ♡10. Neither of those chances was very substantial. What if East held three or more hearts in addition to his spade suit? A major-suit squeeze wouldn't be possible because East sat over the dummy. No, wait a moment. Surely this was the situation where a trump squeeze might work!

Dr Gorse played six rounds of trumps, throwing two spades and two hearts from dummy. The two top clubs, followed by a heart to dummy's ace, left this end position:

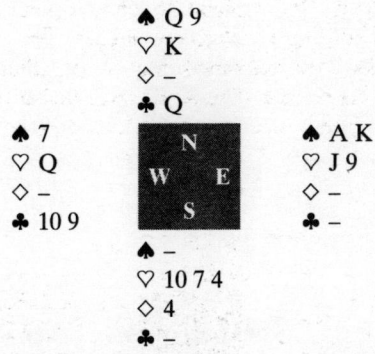

'Queen of clubs, please,' said Dr Gorse.

Brother Xavier, sitting East, could not afford to throw another spade or declarer would ruff dummy's queen good. He therefore released ♡9. After throwing a heart from his own hand, Dr Gorse cashed dummy's king of hearts, dropping the queen and the jack. He then ruffed a spade to his hand and claimed the last trick with the established ♡10. The grand slam had been made.

The Abbot surveyed the declarer suspiciously. That was a trump squeeze, wasn't it? How on earth could an unknown performer, with little or no experience of the game, perform at such a high level?

Brother Xavier leaned forward. 'A heart lead beats it, Abbot,' he said. 'He needed one heart entry to reach the squeeze card, the queen of clubs. The other had to be there to reach the long spade, if I discarded a spade at the end.'

The Abbot reached wearily for his scorecard. How many times had he told Xavier not to make such futile remarks?

'I could tell by looking at my hand that a heart lead might be disastrous,' said Dr Gorse. 'That's why I jumped straight to the grand, rather than give them any further information.'

Dr Moore adjusted his silver-rimmed spectacles. 'Excellent diagnosis, partner,' he said.

The Abbot surveyed the declarer disapprovingly. What bad manners to wear such a worn pullover for a league match against top-class opposition. As for leaping straight to a grand slam when holding four small hearts, it was the action of some teenager trying to prove how clever he was.

The first half ended with Dr Gorse in a tricky heart game.

```
North-South Game        ♠ 6 4
Dealer West             ♡ 8 4 2
                        ◇ J 7 6 2
                        ♣ 8 7 6 2

  ♠ 10 5 3          N          ♠ J 9 8 7 2
  ♡ A 6                        ♡ 7 3
  ◇ K Q 9      W       E       ◇ 10 4 3
  ♣ A K Q 10 3      S          ♣ J 9 4

                        ♠ A K Q
                        ♡ K Q J 10 9 5
                        ◇ A 8 5
                        ♣ 5
```

WEST	NORTH	EAST	SOUTH
The	*Dr*	*Brother*	*Dr*
Abbot	*Moore*	*Xavier*	*Gorse*
1♣	Pass	Pass	Dble
Rdble	1◇	Pass	4♡
All Pass			

Since as little as the ◇Q in dummy might be enough for game, Dr. Gorse leapt all the way to Four Hearts on the second round.

The Abbot led the ♣K and continued with the club ace. Declarer ruffed with the nine and played the king of trumps to West's ace. Not wishing to aid declarer's passage towards an elimination ending, the Abbot exited with his remaining trump rather than playing another club. 'Eight of hearts, please,' said Dr. Gorse.

The 2-2 trump break was welcome news. Declarer ruffed another club in the South hand and then played three rounds of spades, throwing dummy's last club. Both black suits had been eliminated and these cards remained:

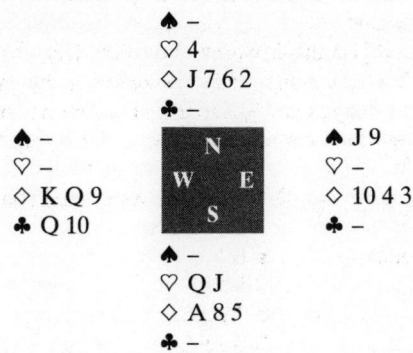

```
                    ♠ –
                    ♡ 4
                    ◇ J 7 6 2
                    ♣ –
   ♠ –                              ♠ J 9
   ♡ –                              ♡ –
   ◇ K Q 9                          ◇ 10 4 3
   ♣ Q 10                           ♣ –
                    ♠ –
                    ♡ Q J
                    ◇ A 8 5
                    ♣ –
```

There was no escape for the Abbot in the West seat. When a low diamond was led towards dummy, he had to win with one honour and lead away from the other. Dummy's ◇J became declarer's tenth trick and the game was made.

'Was it right to take the first trump, Abbot?' asked Brother Xavier. 'If you duck he can't win the second round in dummy.'

Not for the first time the Abbot wondered what Xavier's purpose was, playing in matches such as these. Did he want to win, like the rest of them, or was his whole purpose to seek double-dummy flaws in his partner's play?

'I don't think that makes any difference,' said Dr. Gorse. 'If your partner ducks the ace of trumps, I can play my three spade winners before leading a second round of trumps. He would have to play a club himself and the same end position would arise.'

'Did you follow that, Xavier?' asked the Abbot. 'If holding up the trump ace would beat the contract I would have held it up. I can't even remember the last time I let through a game contract.'

'It was the second club that cost you,' Dr Gorse continued. 'Switch to a major at Trick 2 and I can't eliminate the clubs.'

The Abbot sat back in his chair. He was surrounded by Brother Xaviers! He himself made it a firm rule never to criticise the play of others. These lesser players would do well to follow his example.

The half-time comparison found the monastery 15 IMPs adrift.

'That's surprising,' said Brother Lucius, checking his arithmetic for the second time. 'Did their other pair play well against you?'

'They played all right,' Brother Xavier replied. 'It was a couple of defences that cost us.'

'Don't worry, Abbot,' said Brother Paulo. 'We will put them under pressure in the second half. I will overbid on every hand.'

'That's just what we need,' replied the Abbot. 'We lose the match 20-0 and find we get relegated at the end of the season.'

'It will not be mattering if you don't intend to play in the league next year,' retorted the Italian.

The second half saw the Abbot facing Cedric Parrott, a retired accountant, and his homely wife. Pam Parrott smiled at the Abbot. 'I trust your team-mates didn't give you a tough time,' she said. 'Always a difficult business, defending high-level contracts.'

'They were mainly apologising for their own poor efforts,' replied the Abbot. 'I thought we'd be well in the lead, I must say.'

The second half started with this game in no-trumps:

```
Love all                    ♠ 4
Dealer South                ♡ Q J 10 5 4
                            ◇ A J 10 8 3
                            ♣ A 3
        ♠ K                              ♠ 10 9 6 5 3 2
        ♡ A 8 7         N                ♡ 9 6 3 2
        ◇ K 7 6      W       E           ◇ Q 5
        ♣ K 9 8 7 4 2     S              ♣ 6
                            ♠ A Q J 8 7
                            ♡ K
                            ◇ 9 4 2
                            ♣ Q J 10 5
```

WEST	NORTH	EAST	SOUTH
Brother	Cedric	The	Pam
Xavier	Parrott	Abbot	Parrott
–	–	–	1♠
2♣	2♡	Pass	2♠
Pass	3◇	Pass	3NT
All Pass			

Brother Xavier led his fourth-best club and Mrs Parrott won in hand with the ten. A diamond to the jack and queen left the Abbot on play. Expecting his partner to hold a singleton spade honour, he returned an innocent ♠2 in the hope that declarer would finesse.

If declarer had risen with the ace and repeated the diamond finesse, she would have made the game easily – even if the spade king did not fall. Pam Parrott had fixed ideas of how to play an ace-queen combination, however. She tried her luck with the queen and gave a disappointed shake of the head when this lost to the king.

The Abbot smirked inwardly. His clever move had paid off handsomely. If these opponents thought that a modest half-time lead would carry them to victory, they would be sadly disappointed.

Brother Xavier returned a club, removing dummy's ace, and declarer played a heart to the king. Xavier could see that there was no future in holding up the ace. Declarer would be in hand to score any spade winners she had and would then be able to finesse again in diamonds. He won the first round of hearts with the ace and returned a heart to lock the lead in dummy. These cards remained:

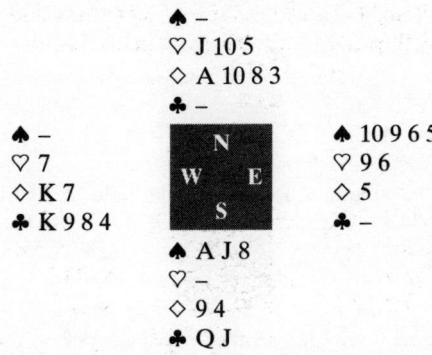

```
              ♠ –
              ♡ J 10 5
              ◇ A 10 8 3
              ♣ –
  ♠ –                        ♠ 10 9 6 5
  ♡ 7          N             ♡ 9 6
  ◇ K 7     W     E          ◇ 5
  ♣ K 9 8 4      S           ♣ –
              ♠ A J 8
              ♡ –
              ◇ 9 4
              ♣ Q J
```

Pam Parrott surveyed the scene unhappily. Oh dear, she had ended up in the wrong hand. It seemed to happen to her quite often nowadays.

The Abbot sat back contentedly in his chair. Fancy playing yourself off in a cold game! The old dear could easily have made the contract by putting up the spade ace. She would probably think for ages now – much too late, of course – and eventually be forced to play for the drop in diamonds. It was pathetic.

Suddenly the Abbot blinked. Good gracious, it seemed she could make the contract by cashing the jack of hearts and throwing him in with a low heart! He would then have to lead a diamond into dummy's tenace, giving her the whole suit, or a spade to the South hand, permitting a second diamond finesse. Had he missed the chance to unblock in hearts? He must have done. How incredibly careless! Playing in a top-class event, such a defence would have been automatic for a player of his calibre. It was difficult to give a full effort, playing in these silly minor leagues.

'Sorry, Cedric,' said Mrs Parrott. 'I think I've messed this one up.'

The Abbot breathed a sigh of relief. The old dear hadn't seen the throw-in! That was a let off.

'Jack of hearts,' said Mrs Parrott.

The Abbot contributed a belated nine to this trick.

'And another heart,' said Mrs Parrott.

Her husband, not overjoyed that his wife had misplayed yet another hand, leaned forward and played the five of hearts.

The Abbot's mouth fell open. 'No, no!' he exclaimed. 'Your wife surely meant to play the ten of hearts. The five of hearts isn't good. Look, I have the six.'

Cedric Parrott closed his eyes for a moment. Two mis-plays on one deal! That was pushing it a bit, even for Pam. 'It's too late now,' he said. 'The card has been played.'

Light had dawned on Mrs Parrott. This low heart might not be such a bad idea – the Abbot would have to help her with his return. 'I meant to play a low heart anyway,' she declared. 'There's no need to change it.'

With a weary expression the Abbot won with the six. He returned a diamond, in the desperate hope that Xavier held four cards in the suit. It was not to be. Dummy's remaining cards proved to be good and the game was made.

'Didn't you have a lower heart to keep, Abbot?' asked Brother Xavier.

'Now I've heard everything,' declared the Abbot. 'You misdefend yourself, then put the blame on me.'

Brother Xavier looked blankly across the table.

'Have you never heard of protecting your partner?' continued the Abbot. 'Cash the king of clubs before you exit in hearts and the contract has no chance, whatever hearts I hold. Declarer will have lost four tricks already and can't afford to lose a further heart.'

Not long afterwards, the Parrotts were standing in their front hall, bidding the monastery team farewell. They had won the match 16-4, their first win of the season.

'I thought your team was bottom of the league,' said the Abbot, who was having some difficulty with the buttons on his coat. 'There must be some mistake on the web-site that displays the league tables.'

'No, that's perfectly correct,' Cedric Parrott replied. 'The two doctors are usually on call during the night and can hardly ever play. In the first four matches we had Ronnie and Olive Cutforth as our other pair.'

The Abbot abandoned the last few buttons and reached for his car keys. Surely there should be some rule about varying the strength of your team. Playing against the Cutforths, it would be physically impossible to avoid a 20-0 win.

'See you next year!' said Mrs Parrott, waving cheerily as the monastery team disappeared into the darkness.

The Abbot peered through the light drizzle, trying to locate his car. 'I wouldn't bank on it,' he said.

19.   The Abbot's Great Sacrifice

The monastery heat of the BBL Charity Pairs was nearing its close and the Abbot gazed proudly at his scorecard. 'Over 60 percent!' he exclaimed. 'That should be worth a bundle of local points.'

Brother Xavier nodded politely. Yes, another 500 local points would be coming their way. So what? Did anyone except his present partner ever look at the masterpoint totals?

The Abbot's eyes were shining. 'Three near-tops on the last round and we might even figure in the national rankings,' he continued. 'I've played very well tonight, even though I say it myself.'

'Evening, Abbot,' said Brother Cameron, flopping into the East chair.

The Abbot groaned inwardly. Why couldn't some weaker pair have arrived for the last round? Not that Brother Cameron's recent good luck again him could last for ever.

The players drew their cards for this board:

```
East-West game              ♠ K J 7 2
Dealer South                ♡ A Q 8 4 2
                            ◇ 8 4
                            ♣ 7 4
        ♠ 9                     N           ♠ 5 4
        ♡ K 9                               ♡ J 10 7
        ◇ K Q J 7 6 3     W        E        ◇ 10 5 2
        ♣ A Q 8 6             S            ♣ J 10 9 3 2
                            ♠ A Q 10 8 6 3
                            ♡ 6 5 3
                            ◇ A 9
                            ♣ K 5
```

WEST	NORTH	EAST	SOUTH
Brother	*Brother*	*Brother*	*The*
Damien	*Xavier*	*Cameron*	*Abbot*
–	–	–	1♠
2◇	4♠	All Pass	

Brother Damien led the ◇K and down went the dummy. 'I know we play fit-jumps after intervention, Abbot,' said Brother Xavier. 'But I thought it was better to go straight to the four-level.'

'It's fine,' grunted the Abbot. How could he concentrate on the play with Xavier wittering on like that? 'Play low.'

'Would you have preferred Three Hearts instead of Four Spades?' continued Brother Xavier.

'Play low,' said the Abbot again. How many times had he rebuked opponents for prattling on about the bidding? Now his own partner was doing it.

Hoping to keep East off lead, the Abbot allowed the king of diamonds to win the first trick. He won the diamond continuation with the ace and drew trumps in two rounds, West discarding a diamond. A heart to the queen won the next trick and the Abbot returned to his hand with a trump to lead another heart. When the king appeared on his left, he repeated his manoeuvre at Trick 1 – allowing a red king to hold.

Realising that dummy's hearts were good, Brother Damien tried his luck with ace and another club. The Abbot won the second round with the king and claimed ten tricks. 'Appalling defence, Brother Damien,' he declared.

'Was it, Abbot?' said the novice. 'What could I have done?'

'He still hasn't seen it!' exclaimed the Abbot. 'Ditch the king of hearts on the second round of trumps. Then your partner can win the third heart and send a club through. Defend like a human being and I wouldn't have a chance.'

'Yes, I see,' replied Brother Damien. 'That would be a very clever defence.'

The Abbot nodded. 'To someone at your level, yes,' he replied. 'For an experienced player it would be automatic.'

'I'm not sure that defence beats the contract, actually,' said Brother Xavier. 'What if you play one round of hearts, removing West's last heart and then play a low club from both hands?'

'That's what I was thinking,' said Brother Cameron. 'If I win and play a second heart, you can end-play Damien with the king of clubs to the ace and he'll have to give you a ruff-and-discard. If I play a club instead, he's end-played straight away.'

The Abbot had rarely encountered such impudence. 'Did anyone ask your opinion?' he said.

'Sorry, Abbot, I just thought that . . .'

'If players of forty years experience ever need advice from some beginner at the game, they'll ask for it,' declared the Abbot. He turned once more towards Brother Damien. 'Get rid of that king of hearts,' he said. 'That's the lesson of the hand.'

This was the second board of the round:

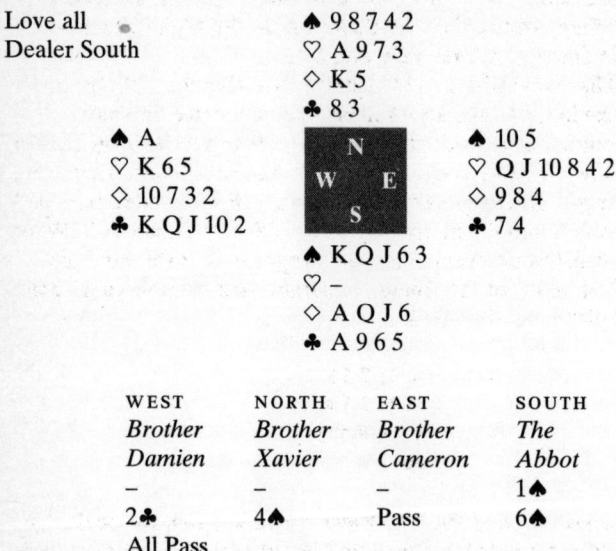

Love all
Dealer South

North: ♠ 9 8 7 4 2 ♡ A 9 7 3 ◇ K 5 ♣ 8 3

West: ♠ A ♡ K 6 5 ◇ 10 7 3 2 ♣ K Q J 10 2

East: ♠ 10 5 ♡ Q J 10 8 4 2 ◇ 9 8 4 ♣ 7 4

South: ♠ K Q J 6 3 ♡ – ◇ A Q J 6 ♣ A 9 6 5

WEST	NORTH	EAST	SOUTH
Brother	*Brother*	*Brother*	*The*
Damien	*Xavier*	*Cameron*	*Abbot*
–	–	–	1♠
2♣	4♠	Pass	6♠
All Pass			

The Abbot lost no time in bidding the spade slam. There was bound to be some play for it or the deal wouldn't have been chosen for a Charity Pairs. In any case, he had a four-loser hand. He was surely full value for a raise to six.

Brother Damien led the king of clubs and down went the dummy. The Abbot winced. No ace of trumps? Surely Xavier should have held that card for a raise to the four-level. Still, if three rounds of diamonds stood up he would be able to get dummy's club loser away.

The Abbot won the club lead and continued with the king, ace and queen of diamonds. Away went dummy's remaining club and no-one ruffed. Breathing a sigh of relief, the Abbot played the queen of trumps. West won with the ace and led the last outstanding diamond.

The Abbot viewed this card with some alarm. West had overcalled in clubs, hadn't he? It was appallingly bad luck that the last diamond should lie with him, rather than with East. 'Throw a heart,' he said.

Brother Cameron ruffed with the ten and the slam was one down.

'That's all I need,' declared the Abbot. 'We bid an excellent slam on just 24 points. Then the cards lie in the only way possible for the defenders to score an overruff.

'Your last diamond winner was a liability, Abbot,' said Brother Xavier. 'Perhaps you could have thrown it on the ace of hearts when you were in dummy with the diamond king.'

'Wow! That would be good,' said Brother Damien. 'To be really fancy you could throw the ace of diamonds on the ace of hearts.'

The Abbot beckoned wearily for the next board to be brought into position. How on earth had he missed it? Against Brother Cameron, too, the biggest gossip known to mankind. An hour after play had finished, everyone in the monastery would have heard about it. What was worse, a fistful of local points had disappeared down the drain.

On the last board of the round, vulnerable against non-vulnerable, the Abbot picked up this hand:

♠ K 7 5 3
♡ K 7 5 4
♢ A K 8 6
♣ 3

'Two Diamonds,' said Brother Xavier, who was first to speak. This was the multi-coloured Two Diamonds, usually based on a weak two in one of the majors.

The Abbot looked down at his hand once more. A vulnerable multi showed a respectable hand, even at pairs. He would respond with the 2NT relay, to find out which suit Xavier held, and then raise to game.

'Three Hearts,' said Brother Cameron, in the second seat.

The Abbot surveyed the novice disapprovingly. Did these youngsters not know the meaning of the word 'Pass'? It was obvious now that Xavier's suit was spades. How much would Three Hearts doubled go for? If he led his singleton club, he could doubtless put Xavier on lead with the spade ace for a club ruff. Two top diamonds and the trump king would make it one down, perhaps two down if Xavier had another side-suit trick. Even two down would be only 300. It was barely possible that the penalty could come to more than the 620 available in spades. 'Four Spades,' said the Abbot.

After two passes the Abbot was surprised to hear a double from Brother Cameron. He was sorely tempted to redouble. Even if Xavier did not hold the ace of spades, he would surely make five spades, two diamonds, the king of hearts sitting over the heart overcall and a club ruff or two. Xavier should have another high card too, if his spades were headed only by the Q-J-10. Still, a vulnerable Four Spades, doubled and made, would be a top anyway. There was no point in advertising his strong hand, giving the youngsters a chance to run.

There was no further bidding and Brother Damien led the ♡9. This was the full deal:

North-South game
Dealer North

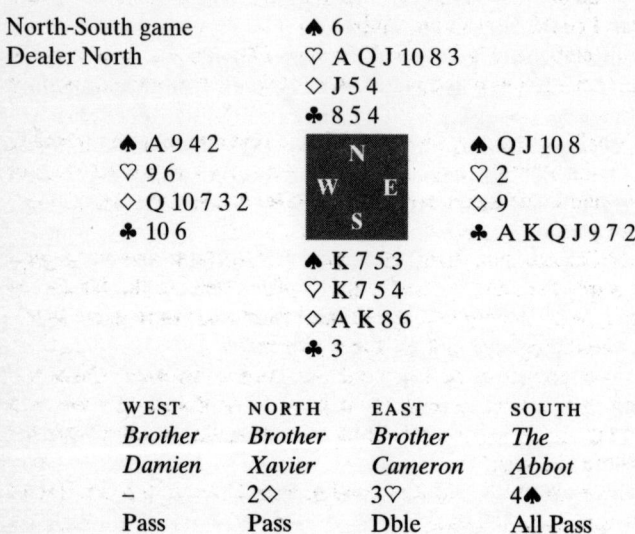

```
                    ♠ 6
                    ♡ A Q J 10 8 3
                    ◇ J 5 4
                    ♣ 8 5 4
   ♠ A 9 4 2                        ♠ Q J 10 8
   ♡ 9 6                            ♡ 2
   ◇ Q 10 7 3 2                     ◇ 9
   ♣ 10 6                           ♣ A K Q J 9 7 2
                    ♠ K 7 5 3
                    ♡ K 7 5 4
                    ◇ A K 8 6
                    ♣ 3
```

WEST	NORTH	EAST	SOUTH
Brother	*Brother*	*Brother*	*The*
Damien	*Xavier*	*Cameron*	*Abbot*
–	2◇	3♡	4♠
Pass	Pass	Dble	All Pass

The Abbot's eyes doubled in size as the dummy went down. 'Did I mis-hear the bidding?' he gasped.

Brother Cameron maintained an innocent expression. 'It was Two Diamonds by North, I said Three Hearts and you went to Four Spades, which I doubled.'

The Abbot blinked. 'Three Hearts wasn't alerted,' he said.

'We play it as natural, Abbot,' said Brother Damien.

'Well, this is ridiculous,' declared the Abbot. 'Why can't you play the game sensibly, like everyone else?'

The Abbot won the heart lead with the king and exited with his singleton club, hoping that the defenders might present him with a club ruff. Brother Cameron overtook his partner's ten of clubs with the jack and switched to the queen of trumps, which held the trick. The jack of trumps won the next trick and the ten of trumps was covered by the Abbot's king and West's ace. After drawing declarer's last trump,

Brother Damien switched back to clubs. The Abbot made a diamond trick at the end but he was eight down doubled for a penalty of 2300.

'Right, you've had your bit of fun,' thundered the Abbot. 'Now you can explain this bid of Three Hearts to me.'

'It's an idea that Brother Lucius was explaining to me,' said Brother Cameron. 'The idea is to confuse the opponents as to which suit the multi is based on. It was fairly safe on my hand because if Three Hearts was raised I could run to Five Clubs.'

'Yes, the club game is cold,' said Brother Damien. So was the spade game, he thought, but perhaps this was not the best moment it point it out.

'I can't believe Brother Lucius would suggest anything so infantile,' continued the Abbot. 'I've never witnessed such appalling lack of respect to one's elders and betters. You haven't heard the last of this, I can assure you.'

Brother Cameron and Brother Damien left the table and made good speed towards the Buttery, where the novices' table in the far corner was already well occupied. Only half-pint beer mugs were in evidence, the pint ones being reserved for the senior monks.

'Have we got a story for you!' exclaimed Brother Cameron, squeezing into a vacant seat. 'You remember Board 21? We had game on but the Abbot sacrificed in a 4-1 fit against us and went for twenty-three big ones.'

'Let's hear about it!' said the blond-haired Brother Stephen. 'Don't leave out any juicy details.'

Brother Cameron feigned reluctance. 'It's difficult to describe a once-in-a-lifetime experience like that,' he said. 'You know, with my mouth being so dry.

The other novices laughed and Brother Stephen rose to his feet. 'OK, I'll get him a beer,' he said. 'I'm relying on you lads. Make sure he doesn't start the story before I get back!'